*Rough
Rider*

Rough Rider

The Life of
THEODORE ROOSEVELT

M. DAVID KEY

NAVAL INSTITUTE PRESS
Annapolis, Maryland

Naval Institute Press
291 Wood Road
Annapolis, MD 21402

© 2013 by M. David Key
All rights reserved. No part of this book may be reproduced or utilized in any form or by any means, electronic or mechanical, including photocopying and recording, or by any information storage and retrieval system, without permission in writing from the publisher.

Library of Congress Cataloging-in-Publication Data
Key, M. David.
  Rough rider : the life of Theodore Roosevelt / M. David Key.
      pages cm
  Includes bibliographical references.
  ISBN 978-0-87021-201-7 (pbk. : alk. paper) — ISBN 978-1-61251-244-0 (ebook) 1. Roosevelt, Theodore, 1858–1919. 2. Presidents—United States—Biography. I. Title.
  E757.K37 2013
  973.91'1092—dc23
  [B]
                                                                    2013033448

♾ Print editions meet the requirements of ANSI/NISO z39.48-1992 (Permanence of Paper).
Printed in the United States of America.

9 8 7 6 5 4 3 2 1

To David Farber, patient adviser,
and
Adam Kane, patient editor

Contents

	Preface	ix
CHAPTER 1	Learning the Ropes	1
CHAPTER 2	Charging the Army	23
CHAPTER 3	Taking Up the White House Burden	47
	Conclusion	79
	Notes	85
	Bibliography	87

Preface

Theodore Roosevelt was born just prior to the start of the Civil War and died just after the end of World War I. The six decades during which he lived saw the United States emerge as one of the world's wealthiest and most powerful nations. That profound alteration in the nation's status came with many growing pains as Americans experienced a multitude of changes in their daily lives. To some extent, the complexities of the era are mirrored in the complex nature of Theodore Roosevelt, a man who helped lead the United States through those changes while hoping to maintain its traditional values as he understood them.

This brief biography of Theodore Roosevelt serves as an introduction to the man and the era in which he lived. It is designed with busy readers in mind, and some complex subject matter has been digested into brief passages. My goal is to engage readers rather than to oversimplify such topics, with the hope of prompting additional exploration into the subject. By necessity, a brief biography omits many fascinating details and analytical points—not to slight them, but to ensure that they are not relegated to mere digressions. The focus here is on the military and political careers of Theodore Roosevelt, and in several places multiple viewpoints have been introduced into the narrative to invite readers to develop their own conclusions. The book is based on the published primary and secondary sources listed in the bibliography, although quotations and footnotes from those sources have been kept to a bare minimum.

Between 1860 and 1920 the United States became a heavily industrialized and increasingly urbanized nation that adapted to major new technologies in transportation and communication as it attracted large populations of immigrants from other continents. A biography of Theodore Roosevelt cannot tell that entire story, but focusing on an individual whose words and deeds were well known and widely discussed during the period can lead to a better understanding of the broader trends. And by focusing particularly on Theodore Roosevelt, we are certain to be entertained in the process.

CHAPTER 1

Learning the Ropes

On October 27, 1858, Martha "Mittie" Roosevelt gave birth to her second child, Theodore Roosevelt Jr., in New York City. Martha hailed from a prominent Georgia family, the Bullochs. She met Theodore Sr. when the young man accompanied his brother-in-law, who was courting Martha's half-sister, on a trip to the South. After their wedding in 1853 the Roosevelts took up residence in a three-story brownstone on East Twentieth Avenue in New York City. Mr. Roosevelt was a successful merchant, particularly of imported glass. Later he turned his energies to banking and was successful in that area as well. The family was not extremely wealthy by New York society standards, but neither did they lack for material comforts.

During his childhood young Teedie, as the family called him, showed few signs that he would become one of the most prominent figures of the post–Civil War generation of Americans who became well-known reformers during the Progressive Era.[1] Recent American history has made much of "the Greatest Generation," Americans who survived the Great Depression, fought in World War II, and subsequently helped move the United States into a position of global leadership. The generation of Progressives is today less famous but is certainly deserving of similar recognition. They too grappled with the effects of a deep and dramatic international depression, global war, and the emergence of a new world order. But while Progressives firmly believed that the United States had a role to play in world affairs, only occasionally did they take an active leadership role beyond the Western Hemisphere. The members of Roosevelt's generation were the first Americans to deal with massive industrialization and an economy increasingly influenced by rapid urbanization. They encountered problems associated with immigration, with highly visible disparities between wealth and poverty, and with new technologies that broke down communication and transportation barriers and led to the creation of a national culture. As he matured, Roosevelt grew to embody his generation's progressive spirit, demonstrating his embrace of the prevailing attitudes of the movement in his political actions. His martial spirit and private intellectual endeavors would be influential in shaping the country and its culture.

The Bullochs and the Roosevelts occupied a specific place in the American social hierarchy. John Adams and Thomas Jefferson perhaps best defined this "natural aristocracy" in a series of letters written to each other late in their lives. Both agreed that the possession of certain traits placed some people above the others, specifically: intelligence, appearance, wealth, virtue, and family name, with appearance and family name being the least important of these. Intelligence produced wealth, but accumulating wealth was mere greed unless the wealth was combined with virtue; that is, with efforts to improve one's community. Mr. and Mrs. Roosevelt, by most accounts a handsome and intelligent couple, were part of America's natural aristocracy both by birth and because of their wealth and their charity work. The Roosevelts came from an old family that traced its roots in America back to the settlement of New Amsterdam. The Bullochs were wealthy southern planters. Charity work was a key part of the Roosevelts' lives. Among other things they helped found the New York Children's Aid Society.

Young Theodore was fortunate to be surrounded by a compassionate family with means. He was a sickly, small child plagued by asthma throughout his youth. His eyesight, always weak, grew worse with age; indeed, at the height of his fame he was completely blind in one eye, although he disguised it so well that few people knew. In spite of the advantages inherent in his family's position, as a young boy he hardly seemed destined for fame, let alone the legendary status he later achieved. The drive and determination that brought him to that level, however, surfaced early. The young Roosevelt used the obstacles imposed by his ailments as a source of motivation; it was a trait that would benefit him throughout his life.

Roosevelt's biographers attribute the development of his personality to his father, and Theodore Jr.'s own assessment was much the same. He received devoted attention from both of his parents as well as his three siblings, the domestic help, doctors, and a series of private tutors. The sickly child was given every advantage in education, and his inventive mind was fascinated by the world around him. He wanted to be a naturalist when he grew up, a plan he maintained until he was in college. He enjoyed collecting insects and classifying plants and animals, and his inability to run and roughhouse with the other children further set him apart. Indeed, his asthma attacks were sometimes so acute that any movement at all was barely possible. When he later recalled his childhood, he remembered most of all his father's presence during those bouts of sickness, as well as his encouragement of young Theodore's quest for knowledge.

The Roosevelt family's wealth helped to enlarge the scope of that quest. During family trips to Europe and Egypt, Theodore visited famous historical and archaeological sites and learned German and some French. Such trips abroad were fairly common for upper-middle-class families of his generation. Indeed, most of the Progressive generation's leaders had "toured the continent" at one time or another as part of their education. These ties to Europe were important to their development of a social conscience. Young Theodore developed similar ties, but his frail physical body was a more pressing concern at the time.

When Theodore was twelve years old, Theodore Sr. explained to him that he alone could create the strong body that nature had denied him, and he devised a strategy to help his son achieve that goal. He planned workouts with light weightlifting, calisthenics, and boxing with a punching bag. The combination of cardiovascular and strength exercises was a good plan, but the nearsighted boy who enjoyed more sedentary activities was not immediately keen on it. That soon changed. One day while he was traveling without his family, two boys teased him until his temper got the better of him and he physically attacked them—only to be met by derisive laughter. The boys did not even bother to hurt him, thus adding lack of injury to insult. But the incident created a new drive in Theodore, and he grimly set to work in his home gymnasium. He was never able to turn himself into a fine physical specimen, despite his hard work, but his subsequent enthusiasm for "the strenuous life" and his brief but very active military career clearly mark this event as an important one in his life.

Theodore's determination to strengthen his body did not diminish his thirst for education. He did not attend school regularly while he was a child, but his family engaged tutors who visited the Roosevelt home and attended to his education. He was bright, and he loved to read. Like many others of his generation, Theodore's interest in natural science was piqued by Charles Darwin's radical theory of evolution, but he never developed an interest in scientific fields that required arithmetic. His travels had given him some knowledge of languages, history, and geography, and that knowledge served him well. Magazines, especially *Our Young Folks*, which featured stories of boys and girls learning lessons in morality, were his favorite reading material, but books that featured animals or adventure were high on his list as well. The lurid "dime novels" popular in the nineteenth century were unwelcome in the Roosevelt home, but he occasionally managed to sneak an illicit read.

Although he lacked much formal education, his natural curiosity combined with the work of his tutors and family enabled Roosevelt to acquire the level of education necessary to enter college. He passed the entrance examination for Harvard and joined the class of 1880. He excelled as a college student while never losing his desire to develop physically as well as intellectually. His favorite sport was boxing, and he competed in college tournaments, fighting in the 135-pound class. He was never great in the ring, but he had some memorable moments. Fellow students particularly admired his sportsmanship and work ethic. His other activities included work on the college newspaper, and he achieved membership in Phi Beta Kappa. In his spare time he taught Sunday school. He also grew out his mustache during the Harvard years and met his future wife, Alice Lee, a girl from a well-connected Boston family. After a year of dogged pursuit, he finally convinced her to marry him. Some of the friendships he formed with fellow Harvard students lasted throughout his life, among them Woodbury Kane, a future Rough Rider; Owen Wister, a future novelist; and recent alumnus Henry Cabot Lodge, a future senator.

Although Theodore remembered his Harvard years as an eventful and successful time, he was in some ways disappointed by college. He was frustrated by the curriculum's emphases on rhetoric and debate, especially the requirement to be able to take up either side of a question. "There is no effort to instill sincerity and intensity of conviction," he later complained. "On the contrary, the net result is to make the contestants feel that their convictions have nothing to do with their arguments."[2] And as almost all college students do, he found some of the assignments tedious and irrelevant to his interests. He entered college wanting to pursue a career in the natural sciences, although that course of study was not a path to certain and gainful employment. In his freshman year he discussed his future with his father, who advised him to learn to carefully monitor his expenses if he expected to live on a scientist's income. But along with that warning came his father's blessing and support.

Theodore Sr. passed away the next year, and Theodore Jr. found that science was not what he wanted to study after all. Once he became more familiar with the discipline, he learned that a great deal of the work was done in laboratories rather than in the great outdoors, where he had imagined he would spend his life. He shifted his focus toward the social sciences, but he was not always enthralled by his studies there. An assignment requiring research on the Gracchi, for example, so bored him that it required all of his willpower to complete it. He found recent American history far more to his taste. In fact, as a rising senior he began to write a book about it. By the time he graduated in 1880 he had completed two chapters. By 1882 the two-volume book was in print.

The Naval War of 1812 is generally read today as a curiosity piece because of its author, but among specialists it has a durable reputation for high-quality scholarship. The work represents a remarkable achievement for a historian of any age, let alone a twenty-four-year-old, although the author's youth is evident in his outspoken belligerence in targeting the errors of British historians, and his assessment of the war tends to ignore the Royal Navy's simultaneous concern with Napoleon Bonaparte. Roosevelt assessed the U.S. Navy as only slightly inferior to the British navy, and that was mostly because America had fewer ships. When it came to officers and crews, he declared the U.S. Navy superior, largely because the ships were crewed by men fighting because they chose to enlist rather than because they had been impressed into service. American crews tended to shoot better than their British counterparts and, as important to Roosevelt, fought with more skill and honor. U.S. naval vessels were thus democratic institutions afloat. This assessment places Roosevelt's work within the "Whig history" school, dominant in his day, which generally assumes that human history is a story of relatively continual progress toward individual liberties.

By the time the book was published, Roosevelt had graduated from Harvard, married Alice Lee, and moved back home to New York City. His career plans were still not set. He briefly attended law school at Columbia but dropped out (later he completed the degree at Harvard). Then he began to consider politics, an unusual idea for a young man of his background. The politics of the day tended to be "machines" run by networks of well-connected (but not always well-meaning or well-educated) men. Gentlemen, such as Roosevelt, generally considered a career involving this sordid process to be beneath them. Roosevelt, however, still influenced by his father's teachings, thought of entering politics not only as a career move but also as a means of performing his civic duty.

He began making connections with members of the local Republican Party. Because "local" for him was New York City, the men he met were relatively influential. It cannot be said that the party's leaders took an immediate liking to him. Indeed, it cannot be said that they *ever* took a liking to him. But they could not overlook the opportunities offered by the slender young man with his father's name and reputation and his own Harvard connections. This was particularly the case in the voting district to which Roosevelt belonged, which included extremes of wealth and poverty. The impoverished residents greatly outnumbered the wealthy ones and had a tendency to vote Democrat. Roosevelt's membership in the natural aristocracy would almost certainly mobilize support from other members of his class. "Our organization has lost the confidence of the 'highbrows,'" one of the party's leaders explained. "They have not a great many votes, but their names carry weight and their contributions are invaluable to campaigns. To regain their confidence we are thinking of nominating for member of the legislature young Theodore Roosevelt, who has just returned from Harvard."[3] Roosevelt's candidacy for the state legislature was not much of a gamble for the Republicans, as it turned out. On Election Day in 1881, only a couple of weeks after his twenty-third birthday, Roosevelt easily won his seat. In January 1882 he set out for the state capital in Albany.

Politics in the late nineteenth century tended to be localized. The railroads had begun to tie the country together after the Civil War, but Americans were still far less mobile—and less connected to one another—than they are today. Letters were still the primary form of long-distance communication and might take weeks to reach recipients. Telegrams were necessarily brief and relatively expensive, and were used mostly for emergencies or conveying news of great importance. The telephone, introduced in 1876 as Theodore Roosevelt was entering college, was still decades away from being a common household item. Local issues were thus much more important to isolated American communities than national ones. Presidential campaigns were hotly contested, and elected representatives debated and bickered in Washington, but that was far away for most Americans.

This is not to say that Americans did not care about political issues. Even those living in relative isolation understood that citizenship in a democratic republic entailed a certain level of involvement. But few Americans studied the issues well enough to have a deep knowledge of them. Most adopted a "public opinion" acquired from a biased source. The English politician James Lord Bryce described the process of developing public opinion in his classic commentary *The American Commonwealth*. In urban areas, a man would buy a newspaper and then board a commuter train for work. While riding the train he would read the paper, fixating particularly on the items that interested or affected him, and in that way he would begin acquiring his opinion on an issue. Newspapers at the time tended to be openly partisan and presented the news in a way that supported the editor's views. People read a particular newspaper because it represented how they felt about issues. Thus, our commuter bought the newspaper that tended to represent his own views. That newspaper's opinion helped sustain his belief that his opinion was the correct one. Once he got to work, he discussed his opinion with co-workers, who, largely because they were doing similar work and had similar backgrounds, generally held the same opinion, and so the man's opinion was further substantiated. Individuals generally made political decisions in this fashion rather than by examining two sides of an issue or engaging in civic debate in order to find consensus or possible areas of compromise. In time, Theodore Roosevelt would become a master at manipulating public opinion.

When he arrived in Albany, Roosevelt already understood enough about public opinion to realize that he needed to develop a political style in order to keep opinion on his side. From the start he exhibited flair in his speeches and dress, despite disapproval from his colleagues. Political novices were expected to listen quietly while more experienced legislators made decisions. But Roosevelt argued his points loudly, even to senior members of the legislature. And he was known for overdressing, wearing expensive suits even to informal meetings. The New York City newspapers loved the brash young representative and followed his actions closely, and what the newspapers in New York City reported was followed throughout the state, so that even in that era of localized politics Roosevelt was gaining a reputation that far exceeded his own district.

The state's political machine viewed Roosevelt and his outspoken independence as a threat, and so he was. During his first term he went after a judge whom he deemed corrupt, and he outspokenly refused to support a bill to reduce taxes on an elevated train company. The man the machine politicians viewed as dangerous to their own interests, however, appeared to public opinion as a crusader who fought corruption at the highest levels and stood up to big business and even to his own party leaders. Thus, public opinion deemed Roosevelt a reformer from the very start of his political career, when he was actually just a young man looking to make a career of politics. A political career, of course, required election followed by reelection, so Roosevelt had to balance his efforts to make a name for himself with the wishes of Republican Party leaders. Only they could keep him on the ballot so that the public could reelect him. The balance would soon become too difficult for him to maintain.

New York assemblymen faced annual elections, and Roosevelt was reelected in 1882 and again in '83. Despite his determination to remain in office, however, it would be wrong to depict him as merely a vote-grubbing politician. He did what he could to improve people's lives within his understanding of how that could be done. During the 1880s government and business were generally viewed as separate entities, and the prevailing attitude was that politicians should leave the economy alone. Later in his career Roosevelt would decry that stance, but while in Albany he supported a free market and tended to voice his disapproval of regulation bills as socialistic, even if they were intended to create better working conditions for employees. He even opposed bills giving raises to firefighters and pensions to teachers. His impatience with civilized college-style debates remained, and he tended to argue loudly for his side of an issue and then consider the matter closed. His side was always the right side, and the opposition's was entirely wrong.

Which is not to say that Roosevelt never changed his view on an issue. This happened, for example, after he was exposed to working conditions in the cigar industry. Cigar workers, who lived in some of the worst parts of New York City, rolled cigars in their homes, which were typically vermin-infested tenements. Samuel Gompers, a prominent labor leader known for arguing that what was good for workers was also good for business, persuaded Roosevelt to visit some cigar workers. Roosevelt was so appalled by what he witnessed that he helped push a bill through the legislature that brought an end to the practice and improved working conditions. Grover Cleveland, New York's popular Democratic governor, signed the bill into law.

Interestingly, it was Cleveland who helped bring an end to the first stage of Roosevelt's political career. Cleveland was the Democratic Party's candidate for the presidency in 1884. Roosevelt, who was among New York's delegation at the Republican national convention, supported Senator George Edmunds of Vermont as Cleveland's opponent and was disappointed when Senator James G. Blaine of Maine received the nomination instead. Blaine was a former Speaker of the House and a skillful secretary of state under two different presidents, but he is best remembered today for the chant "Blaine, Blaine, James G. Blaine, the Continental Liar from the State of Maine!" that hounded him during his first presidential bid in 1876. While serving as Speaker of the House, Blaine reportedly sold his influence to a railroad company, and those charges stuck with him (as did the chant) throughout the rest of his career. Almost as bad at the national level, and probably worse in New York, was the revelation that Blaine had referred to Democrats as the party of "rum, Romanism, and rebellion."[4] New Yorkers, who had helped create the Democratic Party back in the days of Andrew Jackson and had maintained a strong Democratic contingent ever since (including during the Civil War), resented the alliterative slur, if not personally then at least on principle.

After Blaine was nominated, several of Roosevelt's friends and supporters moved their support to Cleveland. Roosevelt seriously considered doing so himself but finally decided to stand by the Republican candidate—at a price to his own popularity with the public and the respect of his peers. "He has one idea, and a great many teeth," said one Bostonian dismissively.[5] New York newspapers and magazines, even traditionally Republican ones, opened fire on Blaine, and Roosevelt was in the target zone. He had sided with his party rather than his constituents, unable to maintain the balance that he had sought between those two forces, and it cost him dearly. Roosevelt held out hope through the summer that Cleveland's personal life would turn voters against him, Cleveland being known to have fathered a child with a mistress, but the voters were not swayed. Roosevelt quickly initiated Plan B: run for office from another district. He was eligible to represent a Long Island district because he had bought a house there, and in the autumn he began putting out feelers for support. He found none. Ironically, the 1884 election was pivotal for his young career, but he was not a candidate. In the long run it was probably for the best, but at the moment his political career was in shambles.

The elections of 1884 signaled the end of an era. Americans elected a Democrat to the presidency for the first time since before the Civil War. New York was the deciding factor, and the margin was narrow: Cleveland gained the thirty-six electoral votes that gave him victory on the basis of a thousand-vote majority in New York. By most accounts, Grover Cleveland was a good president—"one of our best Presidents," wrote Owen Wister years later, "too good for his party, as Roosevelt was too good for his; as our best presidents are apt to be."[6] The election also signaled the end of Roosevelt's first period in politics, but he would make a comeback. Interestingly, the Republicans who "bolted" from the party because they could not support Blaine (remembered to history as Mugwumps) cost the Republican Party the election. A similar bolt would have similar results in 1912, but Theodore Roosevelt would lead it.

Roosevelt's greatest loss in 1884 was not political. Months before the election, on Valentine's Day, four years to the day after her engagement to Theodore Roosevelt had been officially announced, Alice Lee Roosevelt died. The kidney ailment responsible for her death (the same that would eventually kill James G. Blaine) had not been previously diagnosed because her pregnancy masked the symptoms. She gave birth to a daughter and two days later succumbed to the illness. About twelve hours prior to Alice's death, downstairs in the same house, Martha Bulloch Roosevelt had died of typhoid fever. Theodore Roosevelt was present at the deaths of both his mother and his wife. Two days later he was present at their funerals. Roosevelt had lost not only his job but his wife and mother as well. He had no reason to stay in New York, and so he left. His baby daughter, also named Alice, was destined to be bright, beautiful, and often at the center of Washington society. But at the time there was no expectation that her widower father would raise her; that job fell to Anna, his older sister.

In *Adventures of Huckleberry Finn*, also published in 1884, Huck concludes his story by saying, "I reckon I got to light out for the Territory ahead of the rest." Mark Twain's Huck spoke with a Missouri drawl much different from Roosevelt's precise New York–Harvard diction, but the two had the same idea. Which territory Huck lit out for is a matter of conjecture, but Roosevelt's is a matter of history—he went to Dakota Territory, in which resided a herd of cattle he had purchased in 1883. But he did not go ahead of the rest, as Huck did. Although Roosevelt could not know it, the great cattle boom days in Dakota were nearly at an end.

The boom began immediately after the Civil War, when veterans returning to Texas found that some five million head of cattle, primarily longhorns, had survived the war. Meanwhile, Union soldiers had helped eat through the midwestern herds, meaning that there were plenty of cattle in Texas and a shortage in Chicago's stockyards. Prosperity was merely a matter of driving them out of Texas north to the railroads in Kansas, a trip for which longhorns were uniquely suited. As the railroads spread across the prairies, however, long cattle drives became less necessary. Furthermore, longhorns are not the best beef cows, and local ranchers had begun producing better beef cattle for the cities in the Northeast and Midwest, as well as supplying government agents with beef for the military and Indian reservations in the West. By the early 1880s, when Roosevelt entered the market, the cattle boom was at its peak. By 1887, when he left Dakota, he had lost more than $50,000 in the venture, one of many ranchers crushed by the boom-and-bust cycle typical of nineteenth-century markets. At least three factors were working against him. First, the boom had attracted so many ranchers that the availability of cattle outstripped the demand for beef. Second, the prairies were simply incapable of sustaining millions of cattle. Finally, the severe winter of 1886–87 killed an estimated 30 percent of the cattle on the range (some ranchers claimed losses of 85 percent), and many of the survivors were injured or weakened and died the following year. Surveying his own losses in the spring of '87 (roughly 60 percent of his herd), Roosevelt rode for three days at one stretch without seeing a living cow.

The fact that the loss of $50,000—slightly more than $1 million in today's currency—did not ruin him gives some idea of the Roosevelt family fortune. But the experience, although costly, was in many ways positive. Roosevelt was happy to be outdoors again. An avid hunter since he was old enough to shoot, Roosevelt enjoyed the big game available in the West. His trophies included grizzly bears, elk, bighorn sheep, and a mountain goat. The latter required a week of hunting on high mountainsides and nearly cost Roosevelt his life when he fell off the trail on a steep slope. Had a tree not broken his fall, he might well have been killed. Roosevelt's boxing skills came in handy in a bar when a man who called him "Four Eyes" (the nickname stuck) insisted that he buy a round of drinks. The bully was drunk and an easy mark, but Roosevelt improved his local reputation by knocking the larger man down with one punch. In another instance, Roosevelt and some companions tracked down three thieves who had stolen a boat from one of his ranches (he had two, the Elkhorn and the Maltese Cross, along the Little Missouri River), and Roosevelt brought them to justice.

Making the most of his Dakota adventures, Roosevelt entered a new and important phase of his life: he became a professional writer. His *Naval War of 1812* had been well received by scholars, but his tales of his life in the West put his work in popular magazines, particularly *The Century*. The magazine's parent company, also named Century, commissioned a book from Roosevelt, published in 1888 under the title *Ranch Life and the Hunting Trail*, and that same year serialized its chapters in the magazine. Century wisely hired the young illustrator Frederic Remington to create the drawings and engravings for the work. The articles were popular, if dry in places, and Remington's work gave them added spice. It can be reasonably said that the Roosevelt and Remington team created the iconic cowboy and launched the western genre. The articles so excited Owen Wister that he began writing his own fiction soon after they appeared. Wister dedicated *The Virginian*, the seminal western novel, to Roosevelt, whom Wister cited as his mentor since their days together at Harvard.

While Wister fixated on Roosevelt's cowboys, Roosevelt's own writings often indicated a desire to fulfill his childhood ambition to be a natural scientist working in the great outdoors. When writing about grizzly bears, for instance, Roosevelt tempered adventure with science: "It is no easy task to determine how many species or varieties of bear actually do exist in the United States, and I can not even say without doubt that a very large set of skins and skulls would not show a nearly complete intergradation between the most widely separated individuals." To that he added moral strictures worthy of *Our Young Folks*: "It is, of course, all right to trap bears when they are followed merely as vermin or for the sake of the fur. Occasionally, however, hunters who are out merely for sport adopt this method; but this should never be done."[7] In general, his books were well received. An *Atlantic Monthly* reviewer wrote of Roosevelt and one of his hunting books, "He gives us a great deal of information in a rather easy, desultory fashion, but he is never tedious. He has had no adventures which are very perilous to his readers, although they probably were sufficiently so to him, but he tells his stories in a straightforward and graphic way which makes them always interesting, and at the proper moments exciting."[8] Perhaps most important, these popular works made "Theodore Roosevelt" a widely recognized name.

Although Roosevelt's short pieces and book-length collections of his personal adventures went over well, his longer, more serious works did not. His biography of Thomas Hart Benton disappointed even the author, who discovered how difficult it is for an extremely busy man to immerse himself in the life of another. But he had high hopes for a four-volume work on the American frontier, which he worked on for nearly a decade beginning in 1888. Yet *The Winning of the West* also bears the marks of a busy and increasingly political man. It takes as its subject events and expansion efforts from 1769 to 1807 within the region between the Alleghany and Appalachian Mountains and the Mississippi River. Although Roosevelt extensively researched the subject, his analysis appears hurried, and the work is notable for its inconsistencies and inaccuracies. Roosevelt largely saw the existence and conquest of the frontier in militaristic and expansionist terms, both of which he considered necessary to building a great nation. He used the similar expansion of the Germanic peoples, and even more so the British, to prove his point. Roosevelt saw the United States as the heir to those nations' greatness and the frontier as its parade ground. Roosevelt recognized the sectionalism developing on the frontier, with the settlement of the Old Northwest Territory being more the product of government initiative while the southern frontier reflected individual thrusts into the wilderness. To his further credit, he placed national expansion within the context of European and Native American diplomacy and conflict. The book's reviewers, however, could not forgive the flaws in the details and Roosevelt's attacks on previous histories, which had also been a problem with *The War of 1812*. The *Atlantic Monthly* reviewer panned the first volume at length, writing, "No man, whatever may be his ability or industry,—even if he be a ranchman,—can write history at its best from on horseback."[9] The final volume fared little better. Professor Frederick Jackson Turner, a respected frontier historian, began his assessment with a few kind words but largely disapproved of the work, citing factual errors as well as the author's lack of scholarly detachment. "While one can appreciate the energetic Americanism of Mr. Roosevelt," Turner wrote, "one can also lament that he finds it necessary to use his history as a text for a sermon to a stiff-necked generation."[10] Particularly appalling to Turner was Roosevelt's depiction of Thomas Jefferson's dealings with the French, which in essence accused Jefferson of treason. Indeed, Roosevelt did pen a low opinion of Jefferson and his Democratic followers, at one point even using the word "evil." The side-by-side portrayal of the two men on Mount Rushmore is a seldom-appreciated irony.

But Roosevelt cannot be completely dismissed as a historian. Indeed, he was named president of the prestigious American Historical Association only two years after Frederick Jackson Turner achieved that honor. His body of work is substantial, especially considering all the other careers he was pursuing while writing, and his intelligence is obvious, even if sometimes overshadowed by his enthusiasm. He was not a great intellectual, though. Henry Steele Commager probably assessed Roosevelt correctly when he wrote that "his mind was neither original nor profound but sensitive and receptive," and that he had an "intuitive appreciation of mass psychology."[11] Probably more important, historically speaking, was the masses' intuitive appreciation of Roosevelt. His scholarly writings certainly added to that appreciation, but only when combined with his popular writings on ranching and hunting. That rare combination appealed to a broad array of Americans who seldom agreed on the larger issues. Roosevelt was not the best roper in the West or the best writer in the East, but he was a roper who wrote, and that placed him within both the Scots-Irish frontier tradition and the New England intellectual tradition. He was a gun-toting, Harvard-trained intellectual whose innate sensitivity allowed him to slip rather easily between the good-old-boy and jolly-old-chap networks. That skill may not require the finest of minds, but it does require a rare combination of experiences as well as the enormous energy to make those experiences known to the public, and especially to public opinion. Roosevelt's brief career as a rancher and his rather longer career as a writer are thus crucial elements of his legacy.

The western genre that Roosevelt helped to create portrays "the cowboy" as a gun-slinging loner with personal sense of justice. In fact, cowboys are underpaid blue-collar laborers whose work is so difficult that often their very bone structure is altered by it. It was integral to Roosevelt's future success that he worked alongside such men and earned their respect. No biographer can resist relating that Roosevelt yelled, "Hasten forward quickly there!" to his workers, who got a good chuckle from it. But even if he had to learn to say, "Hurry up!" he was out there with the workers in an obvious leadership role. They laughed, but they hastened forward, too. On more than one occasion Roosevelt voiced his understanding of masculinity as coming from his work on the prairies. "It was a fine, healthy life, too," he remembered. "It taught a man self-reliance, hardihood, and the value of instant decision—in short, the virtues that ought to come from life in the open country."[12] But perhaps as important, he saw common folk at work again. Cowboys were not tenement dwellers trying to eke a living by rolling cigars; they were men he could admire rather than pity. The Dakota prairie was a far different world from New York or Boston, and it did him good to see it, even if for only a couple of years. The "great die-off" winter of 1886–87 was expensive for Roosevelt financially, but he could look back on his time, if not his money, as well spent.

December 1886 was significant for Roosevelt in another way as well. On one of his trips back to New York he had run into a childhood friend, Edith Kermit Carow, and the two enjoyed the reunion so much that they decided to make it a permanent union. Edith was also a member of the natural aristocracy, and shared her new husband's love of books, but she was certainly the quieter and more reserved of the pair. In addition to raising Alice, a toddler by the time they married, the couple had five children over the course of the next decade. At the age of twenty-eight Theodore Roosevelt could already claim "historian," "politician," "rancher," and "popular writer" as occupations, but time would prove that "doting father" was also an apt description.

Even while running his ranches and beginning his popular writing career, Roosevelt did not entirely remove himself from politics. His time out west helped him to recover from his personal and political losses, but it also situated him to reenter the political fray. Roosevelt was not isolated during his years in Dakota; he frequently traveled back to New York, especially during the winter, leaving his land and cattle in the capable hands of his employees. But when he was in Dakota he personally ran his ranches, becoming in the process an exceptional rider and a fine roper while at the same time evolving from an overdressed "dude" into a respected member of the ranching community. He considered taking an active role in Dakota politics as the territory neared statehood, but New York was really his home. In 1886 he became a candidate for mayor of New York City but came in third in a three-man race. In '88 he backed the winner of the presidential election, this time supporting Benjamin Harrison over Grover Cleveland, and that provided the entry he sought.

Cleveland's loss in 1888 can be attributed to two mistakes. The first was his outright attack on the protectionist tariff that Republicans favored. Tariff history may have medicinal value as an insomnia cure, but it is vital to understanding the politics and economics of the period. Before the national income tax was imposed in 1913, the federal government had two primary means of income: the sale of public lands and the tariffs on goods entering and leaving U.S. ports. Land sales tended to profit speculators more than the government, leaving the tariff as the primary source of government income and, consequently, one of the nation's more volatile political issues. Americans living in manufacturing centers, particularly in the Northeast, tended to like higher tariffs because those increased prices on imported goods, thus protecting prices and profits on domestic manufactures and protecting jobs. Voters in rural areas tended to support lower tariffs because they wanted lower prices on manufactured goods and also because they wanted to be able to sell their exportable produce in as many overseas markets as possible. Those markets expand when tariffs are lower. Nations tend to reciprocate their tariff policies, so when the United States has a high import tariff on certain goods, Americans hoping to sell to other countries have to pay similarly high tariffs on their exports. The Republican Party had its roots in the manufacturing centers and had been the party of high tariffs since the days of President Lincoln. The Democratic Party had represented the low tariff interests and had been particularly popular with southern farmers since the days of Andrew Jackson. When Democratic President Cleveland came out strongly in favor of lowering the tariff, he reestablished an old battleground and lost the support of Republicans, including the Mugwumps who had supported him in 1884.

Alone, his stance on the tariff might not have cost Cleveland the election, because an incumbent president usually has an advantage at the polls. But Cleveland made a second mistake in the summer of 1888 by offering to return captured Confederate battle flags to the South as a gesture of reconciliation. The war had been over for twenty-three years, but the animosity it had engendered lingered, and North and South were not yet truly united. The fact that the North was growing increasingly wealthy and the South increasingly impoverished added to the regional rift. When a high-ranking member of the Grand Army of the Republic (GAR) suggested returning the captured flags, a largely symbolic gesture, President Cleveland agreed. The uproar that followed was instantaneous and loud. The GAR, an organization made up exclusively of Union veterans, formed a prominent voting bloc within the Republican Party, and many of them, apparently, had no desire to reconcile with their erstwhile enemy. Even though one of their own had advised Cleveland to return the flags, GAR members came out strongly against Cleveland. The president immediately retracted his order to return the flags (indeed, it would be President Theodore Roosevelt who returned them in 1905), but it was too late. Benjamin Harrison seized the issue and leveraged the GAR's continuing suspicions of Cleveland into victory at the polls. He promised to support a standard pension for Union veterans and their dependents—something Cleveland had blocked because of concerns that it would create a fraud-prone system. The tariff was the central issue of the election, but the promised pension helped rally the GAR and northern sympathy, and Harrison won the election.

Harrison kept his word. The Dependent Pension Act, passed in 1890 under Harrison's administration, initiated a system of pension payments for veterans. But President Harrison made some unpopular decisions as well, including appointing John Wanamaker to the position of postmaster general, a cabinet post at the time. Wanamaker himself was not unpopular, but his immediate firing of some 30,000 postmasters across the country, most of them solely because they were Democrats, caused a commotion. In fact, the practice of replacing people appointed by the previous administration with others who had supported the winning party, known as the spoils system or patronage, was prevalent in the nineteenth century. But Wanamaker's blatant partisanship roused public opinion against the new administration. It was in that atmosphere that Harrison appointed young Theodore Roosevelt to the Civil Service Commission.

The Civil Service Commission had been created precisely to eliminate the spoils system. The bipartisan commission's task was to develop a procedure for hiring government employees that judged the merit rather than the political connections of those who applied for positions. In its first years the commission was relatively weak because its authority covered only newly created positions. As a commissioner Roosevelt worked to strengthen the commission and expand its authority. At the same time his work on the commission helped strengthen his sense of purpose and his convictions about what constituted good government.

He arrived in Washington in the middle of May 1889 to begin earning his $3,500-a-year salary. Wanamaker continued with his housecleaning until the end of May, but Roosevelt and his two fellow commissioners, both Democrats, could do little about it. Only one commissioner remained from Cleveland's administration, and the new appointees, including Roosevelt, had not yet learned their way around Washington or learned how to get things done. But Roosevelt was experienced at gaining the attention of the press, and he had his own pen, as well. He used both to gain the public's attention and was actually able to make civil service issues seem interesting, especially when he began his first big battle at the end of 1890.

On hearing of alleged corruption in the Baltimore postal service, Roosevelt determined to investigate the issue. He learned that the source of the corruption lay chiefly with twenty-five postal employees who had gained their positions under Wanamaker—making them Harrison appointees just like himself. But that did not stop Roosevelt. Taking the matter before the public by taking it before Congress, Roosevelt used the Civil Service Commission to attack Wanamaker's appointments. By extension, the attack was on Wanamaker, a member of Harrison's cabinet. After extensive hearings, the House Civil Service Committee sided with Roosevelt. These events took place in the summer of 1892, another election year, and the scandal played a minor role in the election, which returned Cleveland to the presidency despite Roosevelt's own speeches on behalf of Harrison. But the battle against Wanamaker and for civil service reform was significant in giving Roosevelt a national reputation as a reformer willing even to investigate his own party's leaders.

The great American reform movement was gathering steam during the 1890s. In 1889, as Theodore Roosevelt was arriving in Washington, Jane Addams was opening Hull House, a social-settlement house designed to assist immigrants in poor neighborhoods of Chicago. The fame of her activism became so great that many historians date the beginning of the Progressive Era to that year. Other activists brought social and economic problems to the forefront of public opinion during the 1890s as well. Jacob Riis photographed and wrote about the horrendous conditions in the slums of New York City; Florence Kelley began the National Consumers' League to improve working conditions for women in the garment industry; Eugene Debs organized the American Railways Union for unskilled workers; William Torrey Harris was pursuing his goals of standardized school curricula as John Dewey was exploring new ways to teach every type of child; Walter Rauschenbusch was beginning the Social Gospel movement based on his belief that true Christianity required assisting the poor; and Louis Brandeis began his career as a public advocate opposed to corporate monopoly. Clearly, Americans were responding to the pressures brought on by massive industrialization and the corresponding growth of cities and immigration rates. Millions of workers, most of them unskilled, came to the United States seeking jobs to make their lives better. They crowded into American cities so rapidly that local governments simply could not accommodate their needs. It was left to well-meaning Americans to improve the lives of their new neighbors.

Historians have found the rural response to rapid industrialization easier to trace than the urban response. The rural Populist movement culminated in a large political party in the 1890s that had lasting effects in America, including the federal income tax and direct election of senators (rather than the selection of senators by state legislatures, as the Constitution directs). The urban response to industrialization is generally called the Progressive movement, and the Progressive Party did eventually arise from it (not to ruin the surprise, but Theodore Roosevelt was its first presidential candidate). But in the 1890s, at least, the word "movement" does not seem applicable to it. Historians have certainly tried, linking the various local reformers by biography, religious impulse, and ties to Europe; all have some merit, but none has been able to define a truly cohesive program.

In one of the earliest histories of the Progressive movement Benjamin Parke DeWitt attributed three political factors common to Progressives: (1) They insisted that political corruption be eliminated; (2) they demanded that government respond to the needs of the many rather than those of the few; and (3) they believed that government must be altered in order to deal with social and economic problems rather than only political and legal issues. Roosevelt's work on the Civil Service Commission qualified him to claim the first two traits, and by the time DeWitt wrote his book in 1915, with Roosevelt clearly in mind, the third was also his to claim. But in the 1890s Roosevelt still believed that voluntarism could solve the nation's social problems, especially if the volunteers were college educated. Extolling such people to action, Roosevelt declared that college graduates "owe a positive duty to the community, the neglect of which they cannot excuse on any plea of their private affairs. They are bound to follow understandingly the course of public events; they are bound to try to estimate and form judgment upon public men; and they are bound to act intelligently and effectively in support of the principles which they deem to be right and for the best interests of the country." Active involvement, he said, rather than passive criticism was crucial. "The function of the mere critic is of very subordinate usefulness. It is the doer of deeds who actually counts in the battle for life, and not the man who looks on and says how the fight ought to be fought, without himself sharing the stress and the danger."[13] Jacob Riis, soon to become one of Roosevelt's biggest fans, put it more pithily: "Roosevelt was right when he said that the only one who never makes mistakes is the one who never does anything."[14] But Roosevelt also called for action according to "the principles which [volunteers] deem to be right." Many early Progressive reformers deemed working within a local context to be the right thing. Roosevelt was one of the few who could claim to be working at a national level.

While in Washington Roosevelt enjoyed the company of many famous names, including writers Henry Adams, Richard Harding Davis, and Rudyard Kipling, and he strengthened his political friendships, spending time with old friends such as Henry Cabot Lodge and meeting new ones, including William Howard Taft. In 1892 Grover Cleveland won the presidency again and did not long hesitate to reappoint Roosevelt to the Civil Service Commission. Roosevelt clearly deserved reappointment, having done admirable work helping to rewrite civil service exams to be more job specific, including having those whose jobs required equestrian skills prove they could ride a horse. What began as a relatively weak office gained more influence during his tenure, although certainly not through his work alone. After a few more years of Washington society and work, however, Roosevelt decided to return to New York City after the newly elected mayor asked him to take the position of police commissioner.

In the spring of 1895 Roosevelt took up his position on the police commission. His fellow commissioners quickly elected him president of the commission, and Roosevelt set to work, making certain all the while that he continued to be in the public eye. He accomplished that by going out and patrolling the streets himself, although he was more on the lookout for corrupt policemen than for criminals. It was difficult to tell the two apart at times; New York City policemen were notorious for accepting bribes to supplement their low salaries. Roosevelt's patrols gained notoriety as he popped up unexpectedly in a variety of places, sometimes even wearing a disguise. The old question of *quis custodiet ipsos custodes?* (who watches the watchmen?) had its answer: Theodore Roosevelt. He replaced corrupt and inept policemen with better-quality men who had to pass a civil service exam to prove their skills. The stories of his exploits abound—Jacob Riis alone could have influenced public opinion with them because Roosevelt made certain to personally patrol Mulberry Street, Riis's pet neighborhood, and Riis wrote glowing reports of the commissioner. Even the *New York Times*, careful to avoid sensational stories in the age of yellow journalism, averaged two articles featuring Roosevelt per week throughout his tenure as a police commissioner.

Even long after Roosevelt's death, the idea of a future president patrolling the dangerous streets of New York City continues to capture imaginations. Roosevelt has appeared in a number of mystery novels—he even stars in a few—either roaming the streets chasing bad guys or showing up in the nick of time to aid the real detectives. Authors have enjoyed incorporating Teddyisms in their titles. In the mystery genre, Lawrence Alexander gave us *The Big Stick* and *Speak Softly*. William L. DeAndrea's *The Lunatic Fringe* is in that tradition, as is Mark Schorr's *Bully!* Roosevelt shows up occasionally in Caleb Carr's novels *The Alienist* and *The Angel of Darkness*. When doling out justice, Roosevelt was certainly more Bruce Wayne than Batman, but the image of the gentleman by day, crime fighter by night patrolling the streets of Gotham dates back well before the Batman comic book series, back to the days of Theodore Roosevelt, Police Commissioner.

Roosevelt was not always on friendly terms with his fellow commissioners, and when the opportunity presented itself to leave the position, he took it. But the two years he spent on the New York Police Commission combined with his years on the federal Civil Service Commission provided him with concrete credentials as a political reformer at both local and national levels. Progressive reform was not yet a coherent movement, but when it became one, Theodore Roosevelt would be ready to take his place at its head.

CHAPTER 2

Charging the Army

The presidential election of 1896 pitted Republican William McKinley, hero of Antietam and champion of the high tariff and the gold standard, against the Democrat and Populist candidate, William Jennings Bryan. The election took place in the third year of one of the worst economic depressions on record, and the economy was a central concern. Those who supported the gold standard, or "hard money," believed that a strong, stable currency was necessary for financial security and that every dollar issued should be backed by gold. The Populists argued for a "softer" currency that blended silver into the economy, thus making money and credit more plentiful, and reducing the burden of farm debt. Further, they wanted a national income tax because they believed that farmers and other landowners were disproportionately taxed on their property while wealthy people hid their property in corporations and were not paying their fair share of taxes. A tax on incomes above a relatively high range would to some extent eliminate that injustice. The Populist argument was compelling and was boisterously endorsed by some eccentric personalities, including Ignatius Donnelly, Mary Ellen Lease, and Tom Watson. It was gaining rapidly in popularity as well, particularly in rural areas, so much so that the Democratic Party had begun absorbing the Populists in the 1894 midterm election, when several Democratic candidates voiced pro-silver sentiments.

In essence the Democratic Party, which had long preferred a smaller federal government only minimally involved in the economic sphere, was shifting to support an activist government with the power to regulate and balance the economy. In doing so it was adapting to changing societal needs and becoming a modern liberal party (as opposed to classic liberalism, which emphasized individual rights and liberties, modern liberalism emphasizes equality of individual rights and economic protection). This ideological shift caused something of an identity crisis for Republicans, who were already using the coercive power of the federal government to shape the economy via tariffs and massive land development projects, including railroads and homesteads. Over time, the two liberal parties would define themselves more clearly, with Republicans generally maintaining that government should protect businesses and should be more responsive to taxpayers, and Democrats generally holding the view that government should protect workers and should be more responsive to voters. But those definitions would require a few years to sort out and would continue to alter according to specific needs of the time and various social issues. In the elections of 1896, as the nation moved into the twentieth century, the Democratic Party was already in the process of redefining itself while the Republicans were left to sort out their response. Theodore Roosevelt played a major role in formulating that response.

Roosevelt did not run for office in 1896, but he began lobbying for a position in the McKinley administration soon after McKinley won the close election. Using his good friend Senator Henry Cabot Lodge of Massachusetts as his lobbyist, Roosevelt was able to secure what he considered a prize: the office of assistant secretary of the Navy. Roosevelt had pledged to work tirelessly, even through the hot Potomac summer, if given the post, and he was able to do so both because of his enormous energy and because Secretary of the Navy John D. Long was a man who liked to delegate work and then leave, providing Roosevelt with plenty of leeway in the office and around town.

Roosevelt was a good fit for the position because he was a devoted advocate of a strong navy. His *Naval War of 1812* had made him a noted authority on the history of the service, and the U.S. Navy he praised in that work was the U.S. Navy he wanted on the water—a strong, efficient fighting force. Roosevelt in his later years would advocate maintaining a strong military on behalf of peace, but Roosevelt in his younger years was a war hawk. "Prepare for war and hope for peace" was a popular maxim, but in fact he hoped for war. Fortunately, the assistant secretary of the Navy lacked the power to take America to war.

The U.S. Navy had undergone a number of improvements during the prior decades. It had played an important role in the Civil War, occasionally in intracoastal and riverway clashes but mostly as a coastal blockade force. But the ships that fought in that war were small and weak by the standards of the world's naval powers. Indeed, America had only the twelfth most powerful navy in the world. A nation with two oceans and a large gulf to defend needed more muscle. The work of beefing up the U.S. Navy fell especially to the Navy Department under Secretary William Whitney during the first Cleveland administration. With congressional support, Whitney scrapped the old wooden sailing ships and turned to steam power and steel. The steel was especially important to him, and he insisted that it be American made, prompting innovations and profits in the steel industry as a result (the military-industrial complex is not a twentieth-century invention). The shipbuilding program began with cruisers, in the proud tradition of American frigates, but grew to include battleships and support vessels as well. By the time Whitney stepped down in 1889, the Navy had twenty-two modern vessels either on the water or in production. By the turn of the century the United States had the world's third most powerful navy, behind Germany and far, far behind Great Britain, but ahead of Spain, a point that would soon prove significant.

Whitney was the architect of the improved Navy, but Alfred Thayer Mahan was its philosopher. Mahan persuasively argued that a strong navy was the key to any nation's greatness. In his 1890 classic, *The Influence of Sea Power upon History, 1660–1783*, he used the history and tactics of the British navy to prove his point. The book, which had its origins in a series of lectures at the Naval War College (founded in the 1880s), gained followers both within the Navy and in the general public. Among those in the public sector who read and agreed with Mahan were Theodore Roosevelt and Senator Lodge. Mahan advocated not just a large navy, but a navy with large ships capable of blockading foreign ports and shelling inland targets—a navy centered on battleships. With Whitney's plans creating the ships and Mahan's plans creating the strategies, the U.S. Navy was on the way to becoming a world-class fighting force.

Theodore Roosevelt thus stepped into an administrative position in which clearly defined goals had already been established. He did his duty effectively, employing tactics similar to those he had used while serving on the Civil Service Commission and the New York Police Commission. He focused on putting the best-qualified officers in command, with longevity of service not always being synonymous with best qualified. He created and sent reports to President McKinley, petitioned Congress for more funds, revised codes and regulations, and generally did what his office was required to do to prepare the Navy for conflict. Roosevelt's various remarks in support of war preparedness are today interpreted as those of a burgeoning imperialist leading the United States into overseas wars for wealth and to subjugate people of color. Roosevelt is at least partly to blame for that interpretation; his *Autobiography* more than suggests that he was busy trying to deploy admirals to strategic vantage points while President McKinley hesitated to take action during the Cuba crisis and looked for a peaceful alternative. "The Government was for a long time unwilling to prepare for war," Roosevelt recalled, "because so many honest but misguided men believed that the preparation itself tended to bring on the war. I did not in the least share this feeling, and whenever I was left as Acting Secretary I did everything in my power to put us in readiness."[1]

The Spanish-American War was fought in less time than would be required to read all the books that have been written about it. For the most part, Spain had lost its hold on its old colonial empire during the 1820s, although it still claimed Cuba, Guam, the Philippines, and Puerto Rico. Revolutionaries in Cuba had been attempting to overthrow Spain's control of the island for decades, sometimes with help from U.S. citizens. Another insurrection was taking place even as the McKinley-Bryan race was getting under way. Better organized this time, including having propagandists located in the United States, the revolutionaries began destroying sugar plantations, in which some Americans were heavily invested, in order to gain U.S. support for their cause. Historians debate whether the revolutionaries could have defeated the Spanish without U.S. military aid, but gaining the premier military power in the hemisphere as an ally was certainly bound to help.

The Spanish government responded to the insurrection forcefully, sending General Valeriano Weyler (nicknamed "Butcher" by the yellow journalist press) to bring the situation under control. Weyler reasoned that the insurrectionist forces were being maintained by farmers, and in some cases even *were* farmers, and so began rounding up likely revolutionaries and sympathizers in the countryside and placing them in concentration camps. The fact that women and children were being held in these *reconcentrados* ensured outrage in the United States, and the propagandists made certain that the New York press was informed of every atrocity. With approximately 200,000 deaths in the concentration camps (when the farmers are imprisoned, there is no food for the prisoners), there were plenty of atrocities to report.

In 1897 the Spanish government changed. The new foreign ministry recalled Weyler and made some important concessions toward Cuban autonomy, although short of granting independence. The concessions angered both the revolutionaries, because they did not include independence, and Spanish loyalists in Cuba who believed that Weyler had been doing work necessary to maintain peace on the island. When loyalists rioted in Havana in January 1898, the United States sent the USS *Maine* as a show of force and friendliness. The battleship blew up in Havana harbor on February 15, killing 260 officers and crew. The naval court of inquiry that convened immediately afterward decided that an underwater mine had initiated the explosions on the vessel. The identity of those responsible for the mine was unknown, but the suspects included Spain, the loyalists, and even the revolutionaries, the supposition being that they may have wanted to force the United States into a war with Spain that might free Cuba. In fact, none of these was correct; there was no mine, although the true cause of the explosion did not come to light for many years. The evidence was puzzling because the explosion had broken the hull of the ship outward—a problem explained away at the time by the "it could happen" defense. Decades afterward, however, a new study revealed that the *Maine* had taken on some bad coal in Key West, and that this particular coal had been reported to spontaneously combust. The *Maine* had a design flaw that sealed its doom: its coal was stored close to its ammunition. One combustion led to another, and the *Maine* blew up. In any event, the initial findings placed blame on an outside agent, and infuriated Americans demanded retribution. President McKinley initially was willing to dismiss the matter as an accident, but public opinion forced him to move from making mild demands for an armistice between the Spanish and the Cubans to sending a message to Congress asking for authority to commence a blockade of Cuba—all this before the Spanish had time to properly respond. The Spanish government was facing the same difficulty: popular sentiment there wanted war with the

United States for interfering in Spain's business and sending a warship into Spanish waters.

And so the two sides bumbled into war. McKinley asked for power to blockade ("forcible intervention" was his phrase), and Congress responded by demanding that Spain recognize Cuba's independence and leave the island, and that the president use military force to make these things happen and then allow Cuba to become a free nation. President McKinley ordered the blockade, Spain declared war, and the United States responded with its own declaration of war, making it retroactive to precede Spain's declaration of war. Theodore Roosevelt was thrilled.

The Navy, equipped with new ships, 26,000 officers and crew, and plans from the Naval War College, was ready to go. The Army was a different story. Most of its 30,000 or so troops were stationed in the West and lacked battle experience. They were equipped with old rifles that fired highly visible smoke clouds in addition to bullets, and they lacked tropical-weight uniforms. Congress authorized an increase in the size of the regular Army and called for 200,000 volunteers; fortunately, few of them were needed. The Navy would be front and center in this conflict.

Spain essentially had three fleets: one in the Pacific, one in the Atlantic, and one held in reserve for defense. The United States planned to rely on its Asiatic squadron, in Hong Kong at the time under the command of Commo. George Dewey, to deal with Spain's Pacific fleet. Theodore Roosevelt had cabled Dewey back in February with a reminder of the general plans in event of war with Spain. The message merely reiterated what the Naval War College had already planned and was mostly superfluous, although Roosevelt trumpeted its significance in his *Autobiography*. In the event, Dewey did not follow orders from Roosevelt; he instead responded to orders from his commander in chief and steamed for the Philippines six hundred miles away, with four cruisers and two gunboats. The entrance to Manila Bay was well fortified, and Dewey expected to find that the bay had been thoroughly mined. Should it survive those defenses, the U.S. fleet would come up against the Spanish fleet, which, though older and not as well armed and armored as the American ships, was thought to be larger.

Admiral Patricio Montojo y Pasarón, well aware of Dewey's movements, had prepared to meet him some thirty miles away from Manila Bay in tight Subic Bay, where the Spanish fleet's smaller ships could take refuge behind mines and within the range of support of shore batteries. He planned to force Dewey to do battle there, expend his ammunition, and have to leave without ever approaching Manila. On arriving at Subic, however, the Spanish found that the mines had not been laid and the shore batteries had not been completed, and it was they who had to leave, dropping back toward Manila. The Spanish squadron of ten ships took up position inside the harbor, six miles away from Manila, to await Dewey, Admiral Montojo having apparently decided to do battle there rather than endanger the city. It was nighttime when the American ships arrived. They steamed steadily toward the fortifications guarding the harbor entrance, which only nominally responded, although they were obviously aware of the American fleet's arrival. Once inside the harbor, the American ships steamed single-file deeper into the bay, with Commodore Dewey's flagship, *Olympia*, in the lead. The few mines the ships encountered exploded harmlessly beneath them. Before first light on May 1, the Americans found the Spanish fleet. Dewey gave his famous order to the captain of his flagship: "You may fire when ready, Mr. Gridley," and the one-sided battle was under way.

Beginning at a range of only 5,500 yards, outside the range of most of the shore batteries, the Americans steamed back and forth five times past the Spanish ships, firing with deadly aim at both the shore batteries and the Spanish ships, decreasing the range with each pass, until they were a mere 2,000 yards away from the ships. The gunfire was so intense that at one point the American gunners had to stop firing because the dense smoke on the water prevented them from sighting their targets clearly. Much of the smoke came from burning Spanish ships. During that break, Dewey ordered an ammunition check and sent word for the crews to have their breakfast. On learning that ammunition was still plentiful, he resumed the attack.

When the Spanish struck their colors at 12:15 p.m., three of their ships had already been sunk and the remainder were afire and soon to be put out of their misery. The American ships had taken only minor shell hits, none of which produced significant damage. Casualties were equally lopsided, with the Spanish suffering 161 dead and 210 wounded while the Americans had 9 wounded and none killed. The bay was his, but Dewey could not take the city—he had no means of occupying it. He sent Marines ashore to disable the shore batteries and threatened the city into quiet submission. During negotiations with the Spanish, Commodore Dewey (soon to be Rear Admiral Dewey) asked that the news of the battle be telegraphed back to Hong Kong so it could be relayed to Washington. When his request was refused, Dewey ordered his men to cut the underwater cable in retaliation. He had to dispatch a support ship back to Hong Kong to make the report, so it was May 7, a week later, before reliable accounts of the victory reached Washington.

In the meantime, Theodore Roosevelt had decided to take a more active and personal role in the conflict. The day before the cable from Hong Kong arrived, Roosevelt resigned his position as assistant secretary of the Navy in order to join a regiment of volunteer cavalry. It might seem odd that a man would surrender a position instrumental in planning and implementing the war (at least according to his *Autobiography*) to fight in it—and indeed, many of his friends tried to talk him out of it—but Roosevelt was determined to enlist. His decision might be attributed to a midlife crisis, because he was fast approaching forty, but his biographers have more often suggested a sociopsychological factor from his childhood. Boys of his generation had grown up hearing of the glorious battles of the Civil War but had thus far lacked the opportunity to garner such glory for themselves. Roosevelt was perhaps even more prone to want to fight because his own father had not, out of respect for his wife's southern family. Placed within this context, the younger Roosevelt's many bellicose statements can be read as a desire to share in martial glory and to make up for his father's failure. In other words, the war he really wanted to fight was the last war, the one that ended slavery, and he saw in Cuba an opportunity to free people enslaved by an oppressive regime rather than an opportunity for a territorial grab. From a sociopsychological perspective the idea has some merit. Most Americans were genuinely appalled by the reports from the Cuban concentration camps, and their sympathies combined with their traditional pro-revolution stance (remembering their own Revolution) to create war fever. But Roosevelt was on record as favoring war for expansion as well as for purposes of liberation. Perhaps some combination of these factors explains his actions: he wanted the United States to enter the war for expansion, but he himself wanted to enter the war to experience the glory of the crusade. His *Autobiography* provides grounds for the combination, including the telling statement: "I had always felt that if there were a serious war I wished to be in a position to explain to my children why I did take part in it, and not why I did not take part in it." Those words do support the paternal compensation theory, but he complicated the issue by continuing: "Moreover, I had very deeply felt that it was our duty to free Cuba, and I had publicly expressed this feeling; and when a man takes such a position, he ought to be willing to make his words good by his deeds unless there is some very strong reason to the contrary."[2] Most of his words on the subject shared with family and friends at the time of the war supported the latter perspective. Roosevelt, without the benefit of Freudian psychoanalysis, simply believed that as he had called for the war, he must fight in it; and he preferred to do so on a battlefield rather than from behind a desk, despite his administrative skills and despite the fact that he had no known fighting skills outside a boxing ring or a bar in Dakota Territory.

Indeed, those administrative skills were crucial in his first days as a soldier as he went about acquiring permissions, men, and supplies. But he could not resist one final act before he left office—actually on the day after his resignation came into effect. On learning of Dewey's telegram, Roosevelt hastened forth to a press conference and announced the victory in the Philippines. When Secretary Long arrived later to make the announcement, Roosevelt had already stolen his thunder and departed to begin another career, this one as a Rough Rider.

Officially, the regiment was the 1st Volunteer U.S. Cavalry under the command of Col. Leonard Wood, a volunteer who already had a Medal of Honor to his credit for his work in subduing the final Apache resistance in Arizona Territory, but the press quickly dubbed it "Roosevelt's Rough Riders." The name was fitting. Although largely composed of cowboys from the southwestern territories, it also included several Ivy League notables on its roster, thus encompassing the two traits that made Roosevelt so appealing—the self-made frontiersman and the college-trained natural aristocrat.

Colonel Wood, too, had such qualities, although he was not born into the natural aristocracy. He had attended Harvard Medical School, receiving his M.D. in 1884, two years after Roosevelt graduated. Wood enlisted in the Army and was sent west as a surgeon, but he took command of troops during combat on one occasion when the commander went down and on other occasions carried dispatches through hostile territory. After Geronimo was captured and the Chiricahua resistance ended, Wood returned east. While stationed in Atlanta he worked on another degree at Georgia Tech and coached the football team. Afterward, he was sent to Washington, where he served as physician first to President Cleveland and then to President and Mrs. McKinley and Secretary of War Russell Alger.

Wood and Roosevelt met in Washington in 1897 and became companions because both enjoyed the exercise of walking. Roosevelt recounted that they sometimes kicked a football around for sport. The increasingly pudgy and nearsighted Roosevelt tossing a ball around with the man who led Georgia Tech to its first football victory over the University of Georgia is interesting to picture. The two also shared a growing passion for war with Spain, a topic of which they often spoke. After war was declared, both men attempted to use their connections to gain a commission in the service, but neither was successful until the call went out for volunteers, specifying "frontiersmen" cavalry regiments from the western states and territories. Roosevelt contacted Secretary Alger, who offered him command of one of the regiments—the first of them formed, in fact, and the only one that would see combat. Roosevelt deferred command to his friend Wood, who did not seem entirely satisfied with the arrangement. Perhaps he feared being overshadowed by the robust personality of his second in command. Had each man been given his own regiment that would not have been a problem, but Roosevelt's deference found favor with public opinion, which saw in it wisdom and generosity, and the two men were paired together.

The 1st Volunteer U.S. Cavalry was originally to have comprised men from the remaining four U.S. territories: Arizona, New Mexico, Oklahoma, and Indian Territory. This arrangement had a hidden advantage. Territories did not have elected governors or state constitutions, so no state governor would be able to negate the Army's command of his territory's militia, something that had historically been a problem. In the War of 1812, for instance, a governor had refused to allow his state's militia to participate in a planned invasion of Canada. In any case, the regiment was not technically a militia force, because it was created specifically for the purpose of fighting this war. There was no shortage of volunteers in the territories, which had been preparing for war for months.

Alger's telegram to the territorial governors (Indian Territory did not have an official governor, being subject to direct congressional oversight) excited a great deal of interest, particularly in its directive to gather men who could both ride and shoot. The governors appointed captains, and the captains quickly filled their quotas, turning away many capable volunteers and others not so capable. The rosters indicate that a wide variety of men joined the regiment, most of them listing cowboy or ranchman as their occupation, but with the occasional florist or baker present. When even your florist can ride and shoot, you know you live in a tough town.

San Antonio, Texas, was the training ground for the regiment, and the men began arriving there on May 7, the day the news of Dewey's victory arrived in Washington. Colonel Wood had arrived on May 5, and by the time Lieutenant Colonel Roosevelt arrived on May 15, training was already well under way. Roosevelt (per Wood's orders) had been busy acquiring uniforms, smokeless gunpowder, and cavalry carbines, leveraging Alger's office to cut through the bureaucracy. The Rough Riders could acquire only standard fatigues and not the woolen uniforms in which the Army fought, a point that would work in their favor in muggy Cuba where the lighter fatigues were more comfortable. Roosevelt's own uniform was tailor-made by Brooks Brothers. Wood, meanwhile, was gathering the horses and related equipment as well as the daily supplies necessary to feed and train the men. The equipment was distributed as it arrived, even as the men were learning to move in formation, on foot and in the saddle. The men's attempts to march provided onlookers with some comic moments, but they could certainly ride. Indeed, some of the horses also needed training, and the cowboys enjoyed showing off their bronco-busting skills. The regiment picked up its nickname during this time in San Antonio, a reference to the cowboys' ability to ride those rough horses. The alliteration with "Roosevelt" made for a natural combination and was certainly better than some of the other options ("Teddy's Terrors" and "Wood's Weary Walkers," the latter reflecting the regiment's marching skills). It was also in San Antonio that the Ivy Leaguers joined the regiment, usually after personally contacting Roosevelt. These men also brought a variety of additional job titles to the regiment, including tennis player. In reality, though, the easterners were big and athletic and wanting a fight, and so blended in well with the westerners, most of whom could claim at least the better education in outdoor living. With a little New York militia training in his background to add to his ranching and hunting years, Roosevelt himself could ride and shoot well enough to live up to the regiment's nickname. Even if Lieutenant Colonel Roosevelt had never become President Roosevelt, Roosevelt's Rough Riders were interesting enough, skilled enough, and ultimately successful enough to attract the attention of historians. Although it is sometimes depicted as a mere sideshow in the war, the regiment proved itself a brave and effective fighting force during the few months it existed.

While some reporters watched the Rough Riders, national attention was focused on the Atlantic Ocean and the Spanish fleet steaming toward the Americas. U.S. strategy initially was to maintain a blockade force off Havana under the command of Adm. William Sampson and keep a flying squadron at Hampton Roads commanded by Commo. Winfield Scott Schley, but several factors worked to alter that. Most important, the Spanish force of four cruisers and three destroyers was making its way across the ocean at a slower pace than the Americans had expected, and in fact had seemed to disappear altogether. Many Americans panicked, imagining a surprise attack somewhere on the East Coast. Cities demanded protection, and Commodore Schley's flying squadron was weakened because he had to deploy gunboats to guard harbors. Meanwhile, Admiral Sampson guessed that the Spanish would head for Puerto Rico to coal up and took a handful of the ships blockading Havana and made his way to San Juan. He found no Spanish fleet but gave the city a half-hearted shelling before turning around.

The Spanish ships clearly had to acquire coal at some point prior to arriving at Cuba, but where exactly they would do that was not known; in fact, the Spaniards themselves were not quite certain on that point. They tried Martinique first but were turned away by neutral French authorities. Then the fleet headed to Curaçao, where the Dutch allowed them limited coal and limited time to load it under their policy of neutrality. Slightly refreshed, the Spanish ships steered toward Cuba. The voyage would deplete almost all the coal they had, however, leaving none for an engagement, especially if they moved directly to Havana.

The choice of destination was complicated by the fact that the Spanish government was confidently fighting a war as a European power while the Spanish admiralty knew that the fleet would not survive in maneuvers against the American battleships, even though Admiral Pascual Cervera y Topete had heard that some of Sampson's ships were off the coast of Puerto Rico. This had been the case with the Spanish ships in Manila as well. If there was any way to avoid an open-water conflict with the American battleships, Cervera wanted to discover it. His three options were to head to Havana on Cuba's north coast and take it on the chin from the remaining American blockade ships there; head to Cienfuegos on the southern coast of Cuba for coal, food, and water, with the probability of quick discovery by the Americans; or head to Santiago de Cuba, also on the island's southern coast but the closest of the possibilities. Santiago was the choice, and the Spanish squadron's decision to stop there would dictate the course of the war. The choice completely surprised the Americans. Unfortunately for the Spanish, however, Santiago was ill prepared to refuel the ships, and they were unable to take advantage of the Americans' confusion.

Schley's flying squadron, meanwhile, had moved farther and farther south from Hampton Roads until it had Cienfuegos covered, but from such a cautious distance that Schley was uncertain whether the Spanish squadron was in port. Schley and Sampson were convinced that the Spanish fleet would appear at Havana or Cienfuegos, but their superiors in Washington began urging them to cover Santiago de Cuba. Believing it was a wild goose chase, Schley complied, steamed to Santiago, gave it a cursory glance (the harbor is protected by a rather narrow opening), and turned toward Key West to take on coal. Orders came to stay around Santiago, but Schley responded that coal was more important and continued northward. Exactly why he turned around in mid-voyage is unclear, but he returned to Santiago de Cuba and, on closer inspection, discovered the Spanish squadron. All that remained was to move the larger blockading force from Havana to Santiago. In order to eliminate the possibility of the Spanish escaping in the meantime, the Americans sank a ship in Santiago's channel. The act resulted in a large explosion and created seven new American heroes but was otherwise unsuccessful because the scuttled collier drifted out of the narrow channel and into the harbor before sinking. When Sampson's ships arrived to supplement the blockaders, the Americans tightened the blockade and undertook some onshore activity, sending 650 Marines supported by locals and an offshore barrage to take Guantánamo Bay at the cost of 6 American lives.

The McKinley administration decided that America could not afford to starve the Spanish out and needed a land force to speed matters along—and quickly, because Cuba would become deadlier as the summer progressed. Yellow fever was the biggest fear. Meanwhile, the Spanish public had been horrified to learn of Dewey's victory in Manila Bay, and the government was making motions to counterattack there. The ships Spain had held in reserve were more modern and larger than those Dewey had faced on May 1, and once in the Philippines would have a home field advantage. Further, Spain was approaching other European states for assistance. With the exception of Great Britain, the European states were generally sympathetic to Spain but unwilling to become involved in the conflict, although that might change. To take some edge off Spain's enthusiasm for a counterattack in the Philippines, the U.S. government spread rumors that America intended to attack Cádiz as soon as Cuba was liberated. And to hasten that liberation, the U.S. Army was ordered to Cuba.

The Army was hampered by its own failings. There was a core fighting force of regulars who worked hard and served well, but the Army had not yet had a Whitney or Mahan to devise and implement improvements. Fighting on land was generally considered the forte of every American, and relying on volunteers had worked well in every conflict thus far from Concord to Appomattox Court House. So the Army had not modernized or developed an equivalent to the Naval War College; it had not streamlined the command process from Washington; and it was certainly not prepared to fight overseas. The War Department spent much of its budget, manpower, and matériel preparing the volunteers called up to fight Spain. An estimated 1 million American men answered the call, but the 200,000 or so who were accepted faced supply shortages and even hunger in camp. There were, however, seasoned veterans in two places who were capable of moving on the Spanish in Cuba: the American West, where veterans of the Indian Wars were stationed, and Cuba, where revolutionaries had been fighting the Spanish for years.

Maj. Gen. Rufus Shafter, awarded the Medal of Honor for his heroism during the Civil War, was put in charge of gathering the invasion force in Tampa, Florida. Shafter, nicknamed "Pecos Bill" for his service in the Indian Wars, concentrated on moving his regulars from the West to Florida but had not been told what his objective was aside from, obviously, preparing a force to invade Cuba. He had plenty of time to do that, gathering a force of 25,000 men into the backwater Florida town while his superiors in the War Department debated, discarded, and bickered over plans. Among those gathering in Tampa were Roosevelt's Rough Riders, who had boarded a train in San Antonio on May 29. After a pleasant journey through cheering throngs in southern towns, they arrived on June 2 and 3 at a scene of near chaos. While Tampa had good proximity to Cuba and an excellent and protected bay, it had only one rail line. Traffic on the tracks was enormous and backing up, with men arriving faster than food. The volunteers were greeted rather grumpily by the regulars, but generally everyone minded their manners and kept busy.

The Rough Riders were fortunate to have a relatively brief stay in the town. Shafter finally got a clear objective when word of the Spanish squadron's imprisonment in Santiago de Cuba reached Washington. He was ordered to load his troops onto ships and take them to Santiago de Cuba. There was a flaw in that plan, however; the Army did not have any ships. Shafter scoured the East Coast but could not put together a fleet capable of moving 25,000 men along with their munitions and supplies. The force had to be pared down to about 17,500, and space for horses was at a premium. The Rough Riders found out that they would be unmounted cavalry at about the same time they learned that they would be leaving four companies behind in Tampa. Nobody wanted to be left behind with the horses, and Roosevelt was actually proud to see grown men cry when they learned that they were not among those chosen to go.

Roosevelt is remembered for his charge against the Spanish lines on San Juan Hill, but that might never have happened had he not first charged the U.S. Army. Shafter was facing heavy pressure from the War Department to move. He was already doing everything he could do to hurry the process, even to personally supervising cargo loading on the docks. Finally, apparently fed up, Shafter wired Washington on June 7 that his force would leave the following morning. He sent the telegram at 10 p.m., at which point he had given no official orders to board the transports. Acting essentially on a rumor, Wood and Roosevelt ordered the regiment to head for the train that was supposed to take the men the nine miles from their encampment to the transports. The designated passenger trains were idling, and neither Wood nor Roosevelt could find an officer in charge of boarding. But since the trains were clearly not going anywhere, that did not matter. At around 6 a.m., however, a coal train went by, and so the regiment hopped a freight. They arrived at the docks to find much the same confusion as they had found at the railroad station, a scene Roosevelt later described as a "swarming ant-heap of humanity," but spotted their transport, the *Yucatan*, in the harbor. While Wood commandeered a skiff, boarded the transport, and had it move to the wharf, Roosevelt moved the men forward, pushing past other troops who were "a shade less ready than we were in the matter of individual initiative."[3] Eventually, the U.S. Army was afloat and on its way to Cuba, and the Rough Riders were in the van. After just missing a collision with another ship in Tampa Bay and spending six days in close, cramped quarters, the cowboys who could ride and shoot were elated to see the shores of Cuba.

Admiral Sampson was delighted to see the Army arrive on June 20, and several of his ships fired welcoming salutes. Sampson and Shafter quickly met to decide on a landing site. Sampson suggested Guantánamo Bay as the best choice, but Shafter demurred. The forty-mile march to Santiago de Cuba from that landing would be through tough terrain and would take up time that might push the affair into fever season, a problem that had plagued British troops making a similar march from Guantánamo to Santiago back in the eighteenth century. Sampson had been in touch with the insurrection leader, General Calixto García, and Sampson, Shafter, and García met to decide how to proceed. Shafter favored landing to the west at either Siboney or Daiquiri. Siboney would leave the shorter march, but Daiquiri had a pier capable of handling iron ore freighters—and thus the transports. García said that Spanish troops at Daiquiri numbered about half of those at Siboney, and so Daiquiri was selected.

The hilly jungle terrain in eastern Cuba had stalled the development of railroads or even stable roads there. It was prime real estate for the 30,000 or so Cuban insurrectionists, and García's force took full advantage of it. The Spanish had 150,000 troops on the island versus the 17,500 or so Shafter had brought, but most of the Spanish force was clustered around Havana. The Spanish and rebel forces alike were short of food and ammunition, the American blockade having made that problem more acute. The distance to Santiago from Havana combined with the terrain, rebel activity, and lack of supplies left Santiago virtually cut off from reinforcements. Spanish troops in the area were aware of the Americans' arrival. They were competent jungle fighters and were certainly dangerous, but they were essentially amputated from their larger body.

The pier at Daiquiri was of some help in unloading the invasion force, but less than Shafter had hoped. The Navy helpfully shelled the hills surrounding the site and also fired on Siboney while insurrectionists made a feint to the west of Santiago in an attempt to draw Spanish attention. For whatever reason, the Spanish garrison had abandoned Daiquiri hours before the Army arrived, and the landing was unopposed. It was not a quick or neat affair, however, requiring four days of work. The Rough Riders were ashore by the afternoon of the first day, June 22, with some help from Roosevelt's Navy connections. Although the troops had been forced to leave their horses behind in Tampa, the officers' horses had been allowed. Unloading the horses and mules was undertaken by the simple method of pushing the animals overboard and assuming they would swim toward land. Some did not, and others drowned in the surf. One of Roosevelt's two horses was lost in that manner, but he was pleased that little Texas had made it safely ashore. The landing had some bad moments. One of the most popular of the Rough Riders, Capt. Buckey O'Neill, was nearly crushed against the pier after diving into the water in an unsuccessful attempt to save some soldiers after their boat capsized.

Being among the first ashore meant being among the first to see action. That was not long in coming. The American force had come to fight the Spanish at Santiago, but a sizable Spanish force blocked the way there. The Army commanders learned from their Cuban allies that some 1,500 Spanish troops had gathered on a hill called Las Guásimas on the other side of Siboney behind fortifications of felled trees and rocks. Gen. Joseph "Fighting Joe" Wheeler, a former Confederate cavalry officer, decided to march the unmounted cavalry already on shore to Siboney, and from Siboney to attack Las Guásimas. The Rough Riders were cavalry, and they were certainly unmounted, so they joined the regulars in a tough seven-mile hike along the road, which turned out to be little more than a narrow path in some places.

Although they had no love of marching, the men kept up a strong pace, with Colonel Wood hoping to have them placed at the front of the action. He was successful. Wheeler divided his force of about one thousand men in half, with the Rough Riders making up one-half of a pincer. The regulars found the enemy first and opened fire from a distance with light artillery pieces before moving forward. The Rough Riders, coming up from a different direction, worked their way slowly uphill, losing track of one another as they struggled through the dense foliage. Spanish marksmen saw them and opened fire. I Company, at the front, lost its captain and sergeant within a few minutes. The men were discouraged. The hot, damp jungle was not at all like the glorious Civil War battlefields they had dreamed of as boys. They had trouble locating the enemy and often resorted to firing volleys into likely locations in the hope of hitting someone. After some confusion, the regiment pushed forward. Fortunately, much of the enemy fire went high, and the Rough Riders were able to work their way uphill and force the Spanish from their superior positions even as the regulars pushed the Spanish back from their side. The Army's first sizable battle in Cuba was won.

The Rough Riders suffered eight deaths and thirty-four wounded, but in the process gained their share of longed-for glory. One Rough Rider was hit six times during the affair but continued fighting for half an hour before the seventh bullet sent him to the rear. Capt. Allyn Capron bled to death on the field because he insisted that he be allowed to stay and watch the fight. Colonel Wood amazed the troops by being apparently bulletproof, never stooping to avoid gunfire as he led his horse around during the battle, and telling his men to stop cursing and start shooting. If Army regulars or public opinion had considered the regiment a sideshow prior to Las Guásimas, there was little doubt now that it was a capable fighting force. Reporters following the regiment (and sometimes taking up weapons themselves) made certain that America knew the Rough Riders were the real deal.

After his first battle, Roosevelt had a poor opinion of jungle fighting. He had to fight on foot with his sword tangling up his legs, and some of his men crouched a little too low beneath the overhanging foliage to deserve his accolades. Further, the Spanish were firing and falling back rather than making a stand, which was contrary to his view of how a battle should be fought. But it was also his first firefight, and he kept his head and kept his men moving forward with a purpose, at one point even initiating a brief charge on a building that sheltered enemy troops. Considering that only a month and a half earlier he had been behind a desk in Washington, he did well.

Although Las Guásimas was helpful as a proving ground for the Rough Riders, it was not the Army's major objective. That, of course, was Santiago de Cuba, toward which Shafter began moving his forces as soon as they were ashore. Moving north through the jungle, the army emerged among the grassy hills east of Santiago. The battles here, in more open territory, would be much different from Las Guásimas. Shafter planned to take the heights above the city. This was not Admiral Sampson's preference—he wanted Shafter to attack the coastal fortifications that protected the harbor so the Navy could enter and vanquish the Spanish fleet. But Shafter worked his way inland to El Pozo, a hill from which he could survey the terrain in front of him and behind which he could establish artillery. Some 10,000 Spanish troops were inside the city, augmented by the seamen from the trapped squadron, and some 20,000 more were within (difficult) marching distance. Cuban revolutionaries had most of these 20,000 men pinned down, however, giving Shafter the immediate advantage in numbers. The Spanish still maintained their strongest defenses at the coastal fortifications, believing that those remained the most likely targets, and so there were only about 1,000 Spanish troops directly facing Shafter on the heights. But the Spanish positioned on the hills were protected by trenches, barbed wire, and several blockhouses, and they were supported by artillery and the Spanish ships' guns. While he could be reasonably certain of victory, Shafter was reasonably certain as well that his force would suffer extensive casualties.

The U.S. assault was planned to begin at dawn on July 1, nine arduous days after the landing had begun. The men were short of almost everything, the only supply in abundance being heavy wool uniforms, but the Rough Riders maintained allegiance to their fatigues. They complained loudly of the lack of coffee and tobacco—items Cuba now produces in great quantity. The problems Shafter had faced loading the ships in Tampa had occurred again in unloading them in Cuba, and the supplies that were most needed did not always receive high priority. Sickness was making its presence felt, and with no respect for rank. General Wheeler and Gen. Samuel Young fell ill, as did General Shafter himself. Shafter maintained his command from his tent, but the others had to be replaced. Gen. Samuel S. Sumner took over for Wheeler, and Gen. Leonard Wood, having received an extraordinary promotion from volunteer general to brigadier general, took Young's place. Lt. Col. Theodore Roosevelt was now Col. Theodore Roosevelt and the commander of the Rough Riders.

The San Juan Heights—*las lomas de San Juan*—comprise a series of hills only about a hundred feet in height. A couple of them earned names from the Americans: Kettle Hill, with a sugar-refining vat visible from a distance, stood about two hundred yards slightly to the north and east of San Juan Hill, the highest and apparently best-defended of the hills. To the north of Kettle Hill, and also due north of El Pozo, where Shafter was headquartered, was the small village of El Caney. Spanish forces were almost equally divided between the San Juan Heights and El Caney. Shafter planned to send about 5,000 men under Gen. Henry W. Lawton north to take El Caney, overwhelming the 500 Spaniards there within a couple of hours of their dawn attack. Some 8,000 troops would meanwhile be moving against Spanish positions on the San Juan Heights. The day dawned as the men took their positions, with Lawton attacking first so that after securing El Caney he could move to support the attack on the heights. But Lawton ran into serious trouble against the Spanish defenders, who kept him occupied until after 4 p.m., killing 81 American soldiers and wounding 360 others in the process. The U.S. Army was not yet the fighting force that it would become in the twentieth century, and the Spanish had better rifles and occupied fortified positions. They were veterans who had been fighting insurgents for some time, while many of the Americans had never seen a firefight. Furthermore, the American artillery was essentially useless. Each time one of the 3.2-inch guns was fired, a large plume of smoke rose into the air and provided an excellent target for the Spanish artillery, which took advantage of it.

While Lawton was stalled outside El Caney, U.S. forces began moving on the San Juan Heights. Roosevelt's Rough Riders were assigned to attack Kettle Hill in conjunction with regular troops. The men moved through trees and crossed a stream, facing artillery and sniper fire all the while, before coming to an open area. Confusion among the troops, the expectation that Lawton would take El Caney before they attacked, and simply not knowing the way through the small forest slowed their movement. It was early afternoon by the time the amassed troops broke from the cover of the trees and began running toward their attack points. The order to charge came from Lt. John Miley, Shafter's aide-de-camp and his official representative, and was relayed up and down the line. By the time it came, the men were about to charge anyway, so tired were they of being stationary targets. On hearing the orders, Roosevelt mounted Texas and spurred him to a gallop as his men followed on foot. Roosevelt's charge was fairly brief, however, because he came on some barbed wire and had to dismount to await the arrival of wire cutters. He quickly joined his men in climbing Kettle Hill under enemy fire.

While the Spanish riflemen had been effective at long range, they were less able to defend against an uphill charge because their entrenchments did not allow a clear line of sight down the hills. The Americans were thus fairly safe while climbing but were vulnerable when they crested the hills. Kettle Hill was rather quickly gained because the "Buffalo Soldiers" of the Ninth Cavalry had done much of the work of pushing the Spanish back. The Spanish were apparently intending to fall back anyway—an act hastened by American Gatling gun fire coming up the hill. The absence of defenders did not mean that the hill was safe, because the Spanish atop the other hills, although unable to shoot down their own hills, now had targets at the top of Kettle. The men dropped to the ground and took up position behind the "kettle" and a blockhouse to await the conclusion of the assault on San Juan Hill. But Roosevelt was not satisfied to wait. His orders were to support that assault from Kettle, and the only way to do so was to charge from Kettle.

Roosevelt, who had almost no experience leading men in battle, assumed that when he commenced his charge on San Juan Hill, his men would follow him. Only five did, and three of them had been shot by the time Roosevelt realized his error. Ordering those men to remain where they were—in a dangerously exposed position—he returned to the top of Kettle and gave loud and clear orders for his men to follow him. And so they did, rushing to the top of San Juan Hill even as the Spanish were relinquishing the position. They were still facing fire, however, and Roosevelt did not hesitate when he came upon one unfortunate Spanish soldier at pistol range. The pistol he used to kill the young man had belonged to an officer on the *Maine*—poetic justice in Roosevelt's eyes.

There were now thousands of American troops atop the hills surrounding Santiago de Cuba, providing ample targets for the Spanish riflemen who had fallen back to rear positions as well as to artillery from the city. After a full day of battle there seemed no question of continuing the assault. Instead, officers began sorting out their men and ordering them to entrench. Spanish forces did briefly mount a counterattack, but the Americans halted it quickly, especially when the Gatling gun opened up. The day ended in victory, but with 89 Rough Rider casualties. The American forces suffered 1,385 casualties altogether that day, 205 of those being fatalities; Spanish casualties were 593, of which 215 were fatalities. General Shafter was not yet aware of those numbers; his estimate of American casualties was considerably lower, but even so it seemed extremely high to him considering that he had faced only 1,000 Spaniards. Now he looked down on the entrenched enemy defending the city and worried that the 20,000 other Spanish troops in the region would fall upon his rear, and he did not know what to do. Over the next couple of days his officers counseled him to stand firm and allow them to maintain their positions, and his superiors in Washington were insisting that they do so, but Shafter was still considering removing his forces to a safer distance. Two days after taking the heights, everything changed and Shafter could no longer doubt that he had the upper hand.

On July 3 the Spanish squadron tried to make a break for it. Their hope was to build up a good head of steam in the harbor, hit the ocean at full speed, and swing immediately west in a race for Cienfuegos. They knew that the American Navy tended to close in at night but back off during the day, and so the Spanish decided to start the race under cover of broad daylight. They almost got lucky because several of the blockading Navy ships were off running errands, but while gaining the speed they needed to break out, the Spanish ships emitted so much smoke that the Americans offshore were alerted. Admiral Sampson was en route to Siboney to meet with Shafter at the time, leaving Commodore Schley to face the ships that he had overlooked on his first visit. Schley was in the *Brooklyn*, which was closest to the route the Spanish squadron intended to take in the race to Cienfuegos and was almost rammed by one of them—and when avoiding that collision almost collided with the battleship *Texas*. After that disaster was averted, however, the U.S. squadron's guns were able to turn the Spanish ships into beached and burning hulks within a matter of hours. Only one American was killed and two were wounded during the battle. Spain's hopes, for all intents and purposes, were beached with the squadron. Shafter now clearly had the superior bargaining position, but the Spanish refused to accept his terms of complete surrender. Eventually the two sides settled for the word "capitulation," and the Santiago campaign was complete. That eventuality was several meetings in the making, however, a period during which the Army was left to deal with prisoners and refugees while its own men were only marginally equipped.

As the summer progressed, malaria swept through the troops, wounding more often than killing, but disabling many. The greater fear was the expected arrival of yellow fever, always dangerous but especially deadly for those who were already weakened by malaria. Indeed, by the time the Spanish-American War ended, disease had killed roughly twice as many American soldiers as the Spanish guns did. And, inexplicably, considering the fact that the United States was on a full wartime footing and had unquestioned control of the sea after June 3, U.S. land forces remained relatively isolated on Cuba and supplies and rations were slow in making their way to the island. By late June, with roughly a third of his troops sick, Shafter began exploring options for evacuating his men to higher ground, the belief being that the lower, wetter areas increased the likelihood of illness (this was true, but the mosquito had not yet been isolated as the vector, leaving the belief that the air itself was the source of the problem). Even in more salubrious areas, however, the men continued to weaken.

On August 3 Shafter suddenly informed Washington that he wanted to evacuate his army in favor of replacements. His medical and general officers had convinced him it was necessary. To sustain Shafter's urgent request, his generals co-wrote a report, known as the "round robin" letter at the time, recommending the evacuation of the troops. Col. Theodore Roosevelt wrote yet another report making known *his* recommendation to evacuate. Stories vary as to Roosevelt's motivation in making this gesture, but they generally fall into two categories. One is that the other officers urgently supporting evacuation prompted Roosevelt to write a letter to Washington to voice their opinions, and he did so because he was not a career officer and so risked little in supplementing Shafter's report. The flaw in this view is that the general officers had already written their own letter, the above-mentioned round robin. The other conjecture is that Roosevelt intended to put the pressure of public opinion on the Army by writing a report recommending immediate evacuation and giving it directly to the press. Roosevelt later contended that he wrote the letter with Shafter's blessing, and that Shafter had told him to give it to a reporter—all of which Shafter denied. Whatever the case, Roosevelt's letter made it into the newspapers, as did the round robin, the leak of which is slightly more mysterious. In fact, the War Department had already given the orders to begin the evacuation-and-replacement process on receiving Shafter's initial telegram, and Secretary of War Russell Alger was shocked, angered, and embarrassed to read of the immediate necessity of evacuating the Army from Cuba in the papers while the United States was still in the process of negotiating a peace settlement with Spain. The very public revelation that the Army was horribly weakened by disease could not help that process (it turned out not to have much impact on the proceedings).

Shocked by descriptions of the horrors their troops were suffering in Cuba, the American public turned their anger on the Army. Secretary Alger attempted a counterattack on Roosevelt, whom he considered the chief instigator in the leak, by publishing an earlier report in which the colonel had downplayed the problems of disease. But the newspaper-reading public did not buy the ploy; Roosevelt was the champion of the common soldier over the insensitive (at least) or incompetent (at worst) War Department. And for him, it only got better. The troops in Cuba were to be evacuated to, of all places, Long Island, New York. When Roosevelt arrived there on August 15, he had been in the papers almost constantly since his celebrated act of voluntarism in early May, through his Rough Rider training and up the hills at Las Guásimas and the San Juan Heights, and was thought to have prompted the evacuation and brought the troops back. He was a national hero returning home—just in time for an election.

CHAPTER 3

Taking Up the White House Burden

Colonel Roosevelt returned to New York just as the state's Republican machine was contemplating a gubernatorial candidate. The incumbent governor, John S. Black, was a Republican, but an investigatory committee had discovered roughly a million dollars' worth of malfeasance to associate with his administration in conjunction with public funds slated for improving the Erie Canal, and party leaders had little hope for his reelection. Roosevelt's triumphant arrival on Long Island presented a new possibility. Party leader Chauncey Depew immediately began to plan ways to use Roosevelt's fame to counteract the taint of the "Canal steal." He envisioned himself standing before the convention and saying, "We have nominated for governor a man who has demonstrated in public office and on the battlefield that he is a fighter for the right, and always victorious. If he is selected, you know and we all know from his demonstrated characteristics, courage and ability, that every thief will be caught and punished, and every dollar that can be found restored to the public treasury." Depew would follow that by recounting the story of the Rough Riders at San Juan Hill while the band played the Star-Spangled Banner.[1] The image was too compelling for the other party chiefs to ignore; they quickly approached Roosevelt to discuss his candidacy. He consented just as quickly and began campaigning even as his Rough Riders were mustering out. Indeed, some of his men attended his rallies and enjoyed the reflected adulation of the crowds. Roosevelt was an extraordinarily popular candidate and won the election.

Interestingly, Roosevelt's task was not just to defeat his Democratic rival, Augustus Van Wyck, but also to overcome the influence of the old guard within the Republican Party—the very people who had decided to make him their candidate. Senator Thomas C. Platt, a leader of the New York Republicans, understood the dangers of placing Roosevelt in the governorship. Roosevelt had been a good party member over the years, but he was too colorful and independent-minded for Platt's taste. Platt also understood that in order for Roosevelt to win the election, he needed to campaign against his own party's machine. Roosevelt's victory was thus bittersweet for his party's leaders, whose forebodings about his independence once in office proved out. There were no spectacular showdowns, but Governor Roosevelt tended to gather information and advice from a variety of sources instead of simply turning to "Boss" Platt for instructions. Moderate reforms and improvements coming out of Albany, including a new tax on public utilities that improved state revenues and improvements in workers' conditions and salaries, including increased pay for teachers, kept Roosevelt popular with the voting public. When Governor Roosevelt came up for reelection in 1900, Republican leaders in New York faced a dilemma. They did not want to support him, but the voters did.

Platt's solution to the problem was ingenious: he would rid himself of Roosevelt by sending him to Washington. President William McKinley, also up for reelection in 1900, had not yet named a running mate, his vice president having died in office. Platt decided to make Roosevelt that running mate. There were problems, though. First, McKinley had his own "boss," his friend and campaign manager Senator Marcus Hanna, and neither Hanna nor McKinley was happy with the idea of Roosevelt joining the ticket. Second, when Platt let Roosevelt in on his plan, Roosevelt balked; he did not want to be vice president. The governor of New York had a nice home and a suitable salary, and he was content to remain in that office. Further, he believed, as most politicians did, that becoming vice president signaled the end of a political career, not a beginning. So when he went to Philadelphia as a delegate to the Republican convention, he met with Hanna and informed him that he was not interested in the position. The story might have ended with that meeting, except that political conventions can be unpredictable affairs. The delegates were convinced that McKinley could not win without Roosevelt's help. Hanna, McKinley, and Roosevelt had to come to terms with the inevitable: Roosevelt was simply too popular *not* to put on the ticket. Thus, Platt's gamble paid off, although not wholly because of his actions.

The elections of 1900 revisited the big issue of 1896, with the Republicans wanting to remain on the gold standard while Democrats wanted to introduce silver into the currency. There were new issues, too, however, most stemming from the Spanish-American War and the imperialism it had engendered. Democrats were unhappy that the United States had gained several new territories under the terms of the peace treaty—namely Cuba, Guam, the Philippines, and Puerto Rico—although the status of each had not been decided. The issue involved a fundamental question: Was the United States a nation that could take control of areas with no intention of either creating an independent state or giving full U.S. citizenship rights to the people who lived there? European nations were doing just that in Africa and Asia. They were no longer acquiring territories as colonies— a "New" England or a "New" France—but were gaining possessions to be used for economic gain. Many people in the United States worried that America was following that course—not only with the islands taken from Spain, but also with Hawaii, which had come under U.S. control in 1898. The McKinley administration had been taking steps to develop local autonomy in those areas, but that autonomy would be limited. The president reasoned that if the United States did not continue some claim on the areas, another nation, quite possibly Germany or Japan, would step in.

Furthermore, the war had revealed a shortcoming in America's defenses, most famously with the weeks-long journey of the battleship USS *Oregon* from its station on the West Coast to Cuba, a journey of 14,000 miles that took it all the way around South America. American ships needed a much quicker way to get from one coast to the other. The Republicans were calling for a canal across the Central American isthmus that would address that problem, although they unabashedly admitted that their proposition was for the purpose of expanding American business abroad into new markets. McKinley and Roosevelt ran under the slogan "A full dinner pail" to accentuate their promise of prosperity. Their opponent, once again William Jennings Bryan, claimed that the election came down to a decision between plutocracy and democracy. Americans opted for plutocracy, and McKinley defeated Bryan even more easily than he had in 1896.

In this election Roosevelt was a symbol of youth in the party and martial victory. His Rough Rider hat became a standard prop in his campaign. His ties to the West helped thwart Bryan there, and Roosevelt gained the reputation as a great stump speaker as he toured the western states touting prosperity. The party had no need to regret placing him on the ticket. His energy, charisma, and fame as a military hero helped to bring about victory. But once the election was over, Theodore Roosevelt found himself in a curious position. He was now vice president of the United States, a job he had campaigned for but did not really want.

Senate sessions might have been theatrical affairs had Vice President Roosevelt been given many opportunities to pound his gavel at Senator Platt and Senator Hanna. But he presided over only one brief session after taking office in March 1901. The Senate met to approve McKinley's cabinet appointments and then adjourned for the summer, leaving Roosevelt with little to do. Naturally, he found ways to fill his time. Indeed, he was hiking in the Adirondacks when he received the telegram that summoned him to Buffalo, where President McKinley was dying. An anarchist had shot McKinley on September 6 while the president was shaking hands at an international exposition in Buffalo. McKinley not only survived the attempt but appeared to be recovering until gangrene set in. He died in the early morning hours of September 14, 1901. By late afternoon of that day Roosevelt had taken the oath of office. He announced that he would continue McKinley's policies and retain any cabinet appointees who chose to stay, believing them more loyal to the work than to the man. He then began yet another career, this one as the youngest president of the United States.

"Roosevelt was a marvel of many-sidedness," Chauncey Depew recalled of the president. Depew's assessments of Roosevelt were always mixed, favorable on the surface but tinged with acid beneath. In this case Depew was referring to Roosevelt's lifestyle while in the White House (Roosevelt's name for the executive mansion, and one that has obviously stuck). Depew recalled Roosevelt's boxing, fencing, and equestrian activities with apparent admiration while also relating that the president made important decisions while in the middle of such exercises and that

European diplomats were sometimes injured or made ill by the attempt to keep up with the always energetic Roosevelt.

Roosevelt's enjoyment of the company of intellectuals reflected another of his many sides. White House lunches and dinners brought together authors, scientists, senators, and foreign dignitaries. Such occasions were not always of a highbrow nature, however, because Roosevelt enjoyed telling stories featuring violence and questionable humor. "Mr. Roosevelt was intensely human and rarely tried to conceal his feelings," continued Depew, a statement that also can be read in several ways.[2] Roosevelt's good friend Owen Wister, often a White House guest, was blunter: "His talk at the table in the presence of a dozen people, about conspicuous persons not present, and about acute situations in public affairs, was often wholly comic and perfectly reckless." Wister likened the president to "a school boy let loose on the playground" and remembered that he gained "the habit of holding forth at times when it wasn't necessary." Wister, at least, tried to forgive Roosevelt's boorish behavior by attributing it to the stress of the job, but such behavior was certainly not typical of presidents. Roosevelt shocked some listeners by openly voicing his poor opinion of certain politicians. "You can't imagine a person like McKinley uttering such remarks without first shutting all the doors and windows, and then getting under the table," Wister observed.[3]

President Roosevelt may have intended to retain President McKinley's policies, but, as Wister pointed out, he was not McKinley. The very personality of the White House changed when he moved in. But in some important ways Roosevelt did run the machine that McKinley had built. His ability to create and influence public opinion by managing the news media was one. McKinley had been the first to use a president-specific press corps, but Roosevelt mastered the system. He made it clear to reporters that there was a reciprocal relationship between them: as long as they wrote favorable reports about him they would have plenty to write about, including the occasional top-level, inside information that only he could offer. He made a point of becoming extremely quotable, spouting "bromides" (called "sound bites" in our day) that served the reporters well and often moved public opinion toward his side. Reporters who refused to be part of the reciprocal relationship might find themselves ostracized from Roosevelt's good graces; in some cases the president complained to their editors.

Roosevelt also continued the modernization of the Army begun during the McKinley administration to address the many problems that had emerged during the course of the Spanish-American War. Secretary of War Russell Alger had resigned under criticism at the end of the conflict, and McKinley had put Elihu Root in his place. Root had a struggle in front of him—like most institutions, the Army was reluctant to change—but he had a plan, and he was winning the battle. Root's plan was based on *The Military Policy of the United States*, a manuscript written by Civil War hero Emory Upton that was being circulated within the Army. Root was so taken with Upton's ideas that he eventually wrote a preface for the work and had it posthumously published (Upton had committed suicide more than twenty years earlier). Upton's book became something of an operations manual for the War Department and remained in use for years. In particular, Upton touted a general staff system, less distinction between staff and line officers, increased education in strategy and tactics, and less emphasis on volunteers (who were not volunteers, Upton pointed out, because they traditionally were promised payment and bounties of some type) and state militias in favor of a federally supported national guard. His ideas would do much to professionalize the Army and create specialists in crucial areas.

By the time Roosevelt came into office, Root's reforms were already under way, including expanding West Point and opening the Army War College in the autumn of 1901. Indeed, one of the first political battles of Roosevelt's administration was against Commanding General of the Army Nelson Miles, a popular old-school officer who was balking at Root's changes. When Miles turned to the press to make his criticisms known, he found Roosevelt ready to fight him for public opinion and, if necessary, to invoke another of Upton's dictates: mandatory retirement of officers of a certain age. It was another year before Miles retired, but when he did, Root also retired the office of Commanding General of the Army and replaced it with Army Chief of Staff.

Roosevelt would come to rely heavily on the advice of Root, a friend and fellow New Yorker who would serve as his secretary of state after 1904. But during Roosevelt's first term Root was busy adjusting the culture of the Army's leadership, creating the general staff system as a foundation for such adjustments. Secretary of the Navy John Long continued in his position only briefly after Roosevelt attained the presidency; he offered his resignation to his former assistant secretary in the spring of 1902. Roosevelt replaced him with William Moody and then created a joint staff system under Root and Moody that would enable the Army and the Navy to work more closely together. Although it was an important step toward a stronger national defense, this early version of the Joint Chiefs of Staff had no real authority.

Roosevelt had six Navy secretaries during his time in office, although not, as one might expect, because he micromanaged the Navy. A variety of factors unrelated to problems with the president was responsible for the turnover. The secretary of war position, on the other hand, was more stable, with Root being replaced by William Howard Taft in 1904, and Taft holding the position until 1908, when he began campaigning for the presidency himself.

Roosevelt built on the foundations of the modern White House press corps and modern Army laid by McKinley, a combination that has assisted many a commander in chief since. In other areas, however, President Roosevelt followed the general intent of McKinley's plans but with Rooseveltian alterations. The Panama Canal is a prime example. The idea of an isthmian canal had been around for a long time, and the United States and Great Britain had even established an agreement about it back in 1850. Lessons learned in the Spanish-American War about the need for Navy ships to transit quickly from the West Coast to the East Coast and the acquisition of Hawaii made a canal even more of a necessity, and the Republicans had placed it among the planks of their platform in the 1900 election. But the questions of where, when, and how the canal was to be built remained. A French company had begun to build a canal in Panama in the early 1880s but had gone bankrupt in the process. The New Panama Canal Company purchased the remnants of that company and approached Roosevelt in the hope of selling it to the United States. Roosevelt balked at first because there was no assurance that the canal was feasible in that spot, given that it was to be a sea-level canal in terrain that was notoriously volatile. But when the company reduced its asking price by more than one-half, Roosevelt agreed to the purchase, and Congress subsequently agreed to fund construction.

Soon after Roosevelt had taken office, Secretary of State John Hay concluded a treaty with Great Britain that gave the United States sole authority over the canal in exchange for guaranteeing its neutrality. This left the issue of negotiating with Colombia, in whose territory the canal site lay. Hay did so, receiving favorable terms. The Colombian Senate refused to ratify those terms, however, insisting that the U.S. offer be substantially improved from $10 million to $25 million. The issue was a thorny one. Panama was a province of Colombia, and Colombia's approval was necessary for the canal project to get under way. Or was it? Roosevelt briefly considered sending U.S. forces to take the canal site but instead sat by and watched as Philippe Bunau-Varilla helped initiate a civil war in Panama. Bunau-Varilla was, not coincidentally, an employee of the New Panama Canal Company, and Roosevelt had prior knowledge of the coming uprising from his own sources—two spies working in the region.

As matters were rising to a head, Roosevelt ordered eight U.S. gunboats to Panama to ensure that the violence would not impede the transportation of goods across the isthmus, using a treaty signed with New Granada that predated the existence of the autonomous nation of Colombia, having been signed in the 1840s, as his reason. The arrival of the U.S. ships signaled the start of the revolution, and Roosevelt quickly legitimized Panama's sovereignty with diplomatic recognition. A week later the new nation of Panama signed its first treaty, which gave the United States a long-term lease on the Panama Canal Zone. The U.S. Senate ratified that treaty in February 1904, and the canal, a remarkable achievement of the U.S. Army Corps of Engineers, was open for business ten and a half years later. In 1921, to eliminate any possibility that Colombia would claim the canal, the United States actually paid Colombia the $25 million.

Roosevelt acted swiftly and powerfully in the Panama affair, illustrating the lengths to which he was willing to go to fulfill his goals. There was probably another issue at play as well: always sensitive to anything he perceived as betrayal, Roosevelt believed that Colombia was indebted to the United States for its role in helping stabilize the region, including helping to halt several previous uprisings in Panama. When the Colombian Senate decided to hold out for better terms, Roosevelt decided to teach a lesson in much the same way that he handled the White House press corps.

The commander in chief loved his Navy and enjoyed showing it off. While it continued to grow in size under President Roosevelt, however, the U.S. Navy remained a distant second to the also-expanding British navy. The Royal Navy was the largest in the world, but the U.S. Navy could at least claim to be the largest in the Western Hemisphere. In Roosevelt's view, this meant that the United States no longer needed Britain's help to enforce the Monroe Doctrine, which prohibited European powers from further colonizing the Americas. Indeed, the Monroe Doctrine received new teeth under President Roosevelt. After Venezuela and Santo Domingo ran into debt problems with European nations, which were willing to use force to regain their investments, Roosevelt stepped in and declared that the United States would henceforth serve as an "international police power" against wrongdoers in the Americas. The Roosevelt Corollary both excluded belligerent foreign navies from American waters and effectively turned the Monroe Doctrine from a relatively passive instrument into an aggressive one. Along with the new policy came many new responsibilities.

But Roosevelt was not concerned solely with exhibiting America's military might in the Western Hemisphere. He wanted America to claim its rightful spot as a world power and was very successful at using diplomacy to realize that goal. Indeed, Roosevelt proved to be such an accomplished diplomat that he was awarded the Nobel Peace Prize (roughly eight years after killing a man in battle) for his role in arbitrating an end to the Russo-Japanese War. Admittedly, Roosevelt did not act unselfishly or unilaterally in bringing the two sides to terms. Japan had asked him to take on the role of peacemaker, which he did, convening a peace conference in New Hampshire in 1905 that representatives of both nations attended. In fact, he did not want either Japan or Russia to achieve total victory in the Pacific because that would eliminate the balance of power between the two nations and allow the victor to become a problem for the United States in the Far East—and, potentially, end the multinational trade agreement to keep an "Open Door" in China. Roosevelt also stepped into a European squabble over Morocco in 1906, and his actions were especially significant in gaining Germany's acceptance of Morocco's independence. With the help of John Hay and Elihu Root as secretaries of state, Roosevelt adopted British-style diplomacy tactics, thinking in terms of balances of power and flashing some naval influence from time to time to bolster his authority.

The issue of America as an imperial power remained unresolved. This was not a new chapter in U.S. history; from its very beginnings the republic had been expansive, although largely in North America. During Roosevelt's second term, Indian Territory and Oklahoma Territory were combined into a single state and admitted into the Union. Arizona and New Mexico, home to many of Roosevelt's Rough Riders, retained territorial status until 1912. Westward expansion was generally viewed as colonization, with expectations that the areas acquired and settled would eventually attain statehood and all the rights that entailed. There were no similar expectations for the islands acquired under the peace treaty with Spain, with the exception of the Hawaiian Islands, which became an organized territory of the United States in 1900. The nation's earlier island acquisitions—Midway, Pago Pago, and Wake—were primarily coaling ports, and neither they nor Guam, acquired from the Spanish, were much discussed. Cuba and the Philippines were a different matter. Both were taken via military conquest with the active assistance of native insurgents who were thus, at least nominally, American allies during the war. When Spain relinquished rights to the islands, however, their future autonomy was in doubt.

Because U.S. forces had entered Cuba to help Cubans gain independence, the McKinley administration promised the fulfillment of that goal. Gen. Leonard Wood, the former Rough Rider, was named military governor of the island (quite the leap from volunteer colonel), and he systematically improved Cuba's economic and sanitary situations before allowing Cubans to draw up a constitution. That initial constitution, drawn up while McKinley was president, made Cuba a U.S. military protectorate, with the United States receiving long-term leases on naval and coaling stations (the United States now considers the lease on Guantánamo Bay to be in perpetuity) and Cuba agreeing that the U.S. military could be used to preserve Cuba's independence and generally maintain order. In the spring of 1902, now under Roosevelt's watch, Cuba became independent . . . almost. Not only was the island tied to the United States by its own constitution, it also fell under the purview of the Roosevelt Corollary. Thus, in 1906, when the Cuban presidential election was threatening to devolve into civil war, Roosevelt sent in troops to stabilize the island and Cuba's future. He worried that Cuba would become a haven for revolutionaries and wanted to halt that trend right away—even if Cuba's liberty required another U.S. occupying force. Whatever the irony when this is viewed in retrospect, Roosevelt was proud that America had at least promised independence and given it, something no other imperial power of the age had successfully done.

The Philippines presented a different problem. Where the Cuban revolutionaries had become politicians, the Filipino revolutionaries had remained revolutionaries, simply switching from fighting the Spanish occupiers to fighting the American occupiers. Emilio Aguinaldo, whom the United States initially supported, organized Filipino troops before Spain was expelled and organized the Filipino government afterward. When Aguinaldo learned that sovereignty of the islands had switched from Spain to the United States, he simply declared independence once again and followed that with open conflict with U.S. forces. McKinley sent almost three times more troops against Aguinaldo than he had sent against the Spanish in Cuba. Aguinaldo was captured in the spring of 1901, but widespread fighting continued for a year afterward. Once again, Roosevelt found himself taking charge of McKinley-laid plans, and once again he mostly continued those plans, heeding the report of the Philippine Commission that the Filipinos were not ready for self-governance.

Initially formed to advise the president on issues related to the Philippines, the Philippine Commission was re-formed under the leadership of William Howard Taft and tasked with creating a civilian government for the islands. Taft became governor of the Philippines in something of a dual role because the War Department and Secretary Root oversaw his commission as civilian governor. He served well, assisting the U.S. military forces that were seeking out remaining guerilla activity and building transportation and communications networks. He also built schools to educate Filipino children in the American-approved form of self-government. Children are more easily trained than adults, he reasoned, and children take their lessons home with them—miniature infiltrators of Americanization. Visitors to the 1904 World's Fair in St. Louis saw a replica of one of these schools, complete with Filipino children at work on their lessons, to show how U.S. tax dollars were being spent for the greater good. Taft also worked with the Catholic priests of the islands, winning their favor and in that way gaining the respect of the people. Roosevelt pushed for lenient trade terms with the

Philippines, even though he had to buck his own party. By 1905 Congress had granted lower tariffs on trade with the Philippines and the U.S. market was open to Filipino wares. As Filipinos gained a place on the Philippines Commission, the Roosevelt administration was able to report increasing success in the islands. Where independence had been given suddenly to the Cubans and then almost taken away, it was given slowly to the Filipinos. Indeed, the Philippines did not achieve full independence until 1946, after World War II, although the United States continued to maintain a military presence thereafter.

America's Pacific possessions—Hawaii, the Philippines, Guam, Midway, and Wake—would become major battlefields in World War II, a point that brings us back to the subject of Japan. In the Russo-Japanese War, Japan surprised the West with its military prowess and gained recognition as a major power in the Pacific. At the same time, Japanese immigrants were making their way into the United States in large numbers, particularly on the West Coast, where they were becoming a significant part of the labor force. Organized labor groups felt threatened by the immigrant laborers and pressured the U.S. government to do something about it. The press became involved, alarming Americans with stories of the threat posed to the country by "the Yellow Peril." The issue came to a head in the aftermath of the San Francisco earthquake in 1906 when the city's school board decided to build separate schools for Asian immigrants. The flow of immigrants had not diminished at that point, even though the Japanese government had agreed to restrict emigration to the United States as a result of the protests. Workers simply applied to go to Hawaii or Canada or Mexico, and entered the country from there. The Japanese government protested the school segregation, and Roosevelt intervened. He convinced the San Francisco school board to back off the segregated schools plan, but he also agreed to increase federal control over immigration. In March 1907 Roosevelt issued an executive order providing legal support for stronger control of immigration, assuming that Japan would honor its agreement to control emigration. Meanwhile, the school board's decision not to segregate the public schools did little to ease racial tensions in California, which continued to escalate, rising to violence and even a two-day riot in May. By the summer of 1907 public opinion in both the United States and Japan was tossing around the word "war."

Roosevelt worried that Japan would see California's step away from segregation as weakness on the part of the United States, and that worry increased as Japan did nothing to create a stronger emigration policy. War was not actually likely at the moment, but Roosevelt felt that some exhibition of power was necessary—he was not the kind of man to shut all the doors and windows and crawl under the table, after all. Without consulting his cabinet or addressing Congress (but after consulting with Alfred Thayer Mahan and George Dewey), Roosevelt decided to send the U.S. Navy to make his point. He ordered the U.S. battle fleet, including sixteen battleships, to sail south from their stations on the East Coast and circumnavigate the globe, showing the entire world (and particularly Japan) the might of the U.S. Navy. Nicknamed "the Great White Fleet" because their hulls were painted the Navy's peacetime white, the ships created an international stir. Roosevelt's decision caused a small uproar on the East Coast as well, with some newspapers even calling for Congress to halt appropriations for the voyage lest eastern North America be insufficiently defended. Roosevelt ended that issue by responding that he had enough money to fund the fleet's voyage into the Pacific, "and that if Congress did not choose to appropriate enough money to get the fleet back, why, it would stay in the Pacific."[4] The ships worked their way around South America to San Francisco; then sailed across the Pacific with stops in Australia, the Philippines, and Tokyo; and from there they sailed west through the Indian Ocean, the Suez Canal, the Mediterranean, and back home. Many observers predicted trouble in Tokyo, which they viewed as the target of the whole saber-rattling affair, but Roosevelt insisted that he expected exactly what the fleet received: a gracious welcome. "I believed that Japan would feel as friendly in the matter as we did," he recalled in his memoir, "but that if my expectations had proved mistaken, it would have been proof positive that we were going to be attacked anyhow."[5]

Because friendliness prevailed, it might seem that the Great White Fleet was an anticlimactic affair, but Roosevelt did not see it that way:

> My prime purpose was to impress the American people; and this purpose was fully achieved. The cruise did make a very deep impression abroad; boasting about what we have done does not impress foreign nations at all, except unfavorably, but positive achievement does; and the two American achievements that really impressed foreign people during

the first dozen years of this century were the digging of the Panama Canal and the cruise of the battle fleet around the world. But the impression made on our own people was of far greater consequence. No single thing in the history of the new United States Navy has done as much to stimulate popular interest and belief in it as the world cruise.[6]

Impressing the American people at a time when he was pushing Congress to fund additional battleships shows the mature politician at work. Roosevelt understood how to sway public opinion, and the Great White Fleet was working that angle. During Roosevelt's time in office the Navy built ten new battleships and increased the size of the force from about 25,000 men to 44,500. Congress had appropriated $900 million for the project, an enormous sum at the time, but Roosevelt wanted more, and the voyage of the Great White Fleet was certain to help him get it. The foreign people he wanted to impress included not only the Japanese but European powers as well, including Great Britain and Germany, which were caught up in an ongoing competition to build battleships. The Great White Fleet was a reminder to all of them that the United States was a viable power in any waters, in or out of the Western Hemisphere.

Finally, stimulating popular interest in the Navy was important not only for monetary support but also for what we would now call consumer confidence. The fleet set off in 1907 during an economic downturn. The purpose of the Navy was not only national defense, on which the economy depends, but also to protect American business interests abroad and to keep trade lines open. By flashing America's power to the world, Roosevelt was shoring up consumer confidence at home. Roosevelt's confidence in the Great White Fleet was justified. It accomplished all his goals while never firing a shot in anger.

The Great White Fleet had a positive impact on Japanese-American relations as well. Soon after the fleet left Tokyo in 1908, Ambassador Kogoro Takahira began discussions with Secretary Root. The resultant Root-Takahira Agreement gave the United States some assurance that Japan would respect U.S. sovereignty in the Philippines in exchange for recognition of Japan's similar claims in Korea and Manchuria. By the time that agreement was completed, the elections of 1908 had taken place and Theodore Roosevelt was a lame duck president.

Theodore Roosevelt is often caricatured as a toothy warmonger charging up a hill in his Rough Riders uniform or threatening the globe with a Big Stick. But President Roosevelt was actually a stabilizing force in American diplomacy, a rather surprising point given his reputation for boisterous outbursts and his general war-spawns-virtue outlook. Certainly it helped that he had the likes of Henry Cabot Lodge, Elihu Root, and William Howard Taft—all of them models of dignity—for counsel. But even in that elite circle Roosevelt was a leader, not a follower. He nevertheless welcomed advice, and not just from his friends. Even a critical newspaper or magazine article could set him thinking, and not just about retaliating against the writer. In the end he was his own man, following McKinley's policies but finding ways to administer them so that the United States could fulfill its new roles as imperial power and hemispheric police without weakening itself.

Roosevelt was in no way a pacifist, but his image as a rabid imperialist was happily self-enhanced. No matter the size of the man, the belief that he not only *can* do violence but *wants* to do violence lends a certain element of intimidation to any encounter. Roosevelt was known then, and remains best known now, for his views that "it is only the warlike power of a civilized people that can give peace to the world," and "nations that expand and nations that do not expand may both ultimately go down, but the one leaves heirs and a glorious memory, the other leaves neither."[7] His actions as president, on the other hand, indicate a willingness to fight but not a need to fight, a reasonable stance for one who holds that office.

Roosevelt's broad public appeal lay in his ability to present himself as a representative of both the hard-fighting frontier tradition and the high-thinking intellectual tradition, but he was not an egalitarian. He had complex notions of racial hierarchies, for instance, that led him to use terms like "civilization" and "barbarians" in his speeches. In the broadest terms, "civilization" was defined by military prowess, and as Roosevelt believed that the most powerful nations were those with biological roots in northern Europe, he tended to also believe that individuals descended from the peoples of that area were superior to other races. The word "race" can be confusing here because Roosevelt, and many others of his day, believed that race was created by hereditary traits that were both biologically and culturally transferred through generations. Roosevelt was comfortable speaking of "the English-speaking race" as though it were a unified whole. Something like skin pigment, then, was not the most important factor involved in defining race, because a person of African descent, for instance, could master the English language. For Roosevelt, however, such a person would continue to retain African traits and thus remain in a different race.

Roosevelt's relationship with Booker T. Washington offers an example. Washington was the first African American ever invited to dine in the White House. Roosevelt extended the invitation in 1901 soon after becoming president. But Washington, to Roosevelt's mind, was not representative of African Americans as a whole; he was a new type of man who was leading his race toward civilization. Even so, Roosevelt had not fully considered the implications of the invitation—it seems to have been more about expanding Republican influence among African Americans in the South than any sort of progressive gesture against racism—and privately voiced regret about inviting Professor Washington after public opinion criticized him for it. This despite the fact that Washington was not only a well-educated member of the English-speaking race but was also a proponent of the view that African Americans should gradually prove they deserved equality, a view not unfriendly to Roosevelt's own way of thinking.

Roosevelt's views on race influenced his foreign policy (for instance, in dealing with the "little brown brother" in the Philippines), but they also came into play domestically. An episode that took place in 1906 is a prime example. One night, between eight and twenty soldiers from Fort Brown armed with Springfield rifles allegedly shot up the town of Brownsville, Texas, killing one civilian and wounding two others in the process of their midnight "raid." Local eyewitnesses, apparently with excellent night vision and a willingness to look out their doors and windows while bullets were flying around them, readily recognized the shooters as members of the 25th Infantry because the shooters were black—as were the soldiers of the 25th Infantry. The men of the 25th had only recently arrived in south Texas as replacements for white troops. Brownsville was a segregated town, and its citizens had made known their displeasure that "colored" troops had been stationed there.

The sound of gunfire reached nearby Fort Brown, where soldiers were ordered to leave their bunks and assemble for roll call and weapons distribution. The 25th's (white) officers thus had a record of attendance.

When the mayor of Brownsville presented Fort Brown's commanding officer with the evidence of spent cartridges from Springfield rifles, the CO had the fort's arms and ammunition counted and inspected. No ammunition was missing (up to 200 rounds had been fired in Brownsville), nor was there evidence that any of the rifles had been recently fired. Expert witnesses later testified that completely cleaning the rifles required at least half an hour in bright light and would have been utterly impossible in the dark—that being important because the rifles could only have been cleaned the previous night immediately after the shooting. A grand jury found insufficient evidence to indict any of the soldiers.

Unsatisfied, Roosevelt sent an investigative committee to the scene, and said committee placed more weight on the testimony of the locals than that of the men and officers of the 25th Infantry. Since the entire 25th was claiming innocence in the affair, its men would not—could not—tell the commissioners who among its ranks had done the shootings. This seems to be the part of the affair that got Roosevelt worked up. After he received the commission's report, Roosevelt promptly acted on the report's recommendation that the entire battalion be dishonorably discharged. The report stated that it was evident that some of the soldiers had been involved and that others knew of their involvement but would not admit their knowledge. "The secretive nature of the race, where crimes charged to members of their color is made, is well known," the report added.[8] The fact that Roosevelt did not question that assertion and others like it suggests a willingness to, at times, emphasize biological traits over military prowess when it came to racial issues—for clearly the troops had military might and spoke the English language. Nor did he question the commission's failure to presume the men's innocence, as the law required, or the fact that legal counsel had not been provided to any of the accused. It was this latter issue of justice that became the central concern in the affair, leading to a Senate investigation and, under President Taft, the reinstatement of some of the men. But it was not until the early 1970s that Congress and President Richard Nixon reversed Roosevelt's decision and granted honorable discharges to the (by then mostly deceased) men of the 25th. Roosevelt subsequently claimed that his decision in the Brownsville affair was not about race but about justice, but it was the lack of justice for which the event is remembered as one of President Roosevelt's worst moments. Roosevelt's lack of hesitation in supporting the commission's overtly racist remarks and acting on its recommendations clearly show that his racial beliefs influenced his leadership decisions.

If the Brownsville affair was Roosevelt at his worst, however, he had plenty of domestic accomplishments to validate his place on Mount Rushmore. Probably chief among these is his record as an environmental conservationist. This category, too, finds Roosevelt working in both the hard-fighting frontier tradition and the high-thinking intellectual tradition—Henry David Thoreau going to Walden Pond with a rifle in his hand. On this topic it is helpful to juxtapose Roosevelt with another famous conservationist figure of his day, John Muir. Roosevelt and Muir shared a love for nature, but ultimately for different reasons, as the two clubs founded by the men illustrate. Muir founded the Sierra Club in 1892; Roosevelt the Boone and Crockett Club in 1887, soon after ending his ranching career. The Sierra Club was for hikers and nature lovers. The Boone and Crockett Club was for hunters who happened to be nature lovers. Both clubs were formed during a period of environmentalism that historian Richard White called "monumentalism," meaning that environmentalists tended to see nature as a monument.[9] Building on that description, Muir's view of nature was akin to a cathedral, a place to go for spiritual growth. Roosevelt viewed nature more as a sports arena—sports being for Roosevelt no trivial entertainment but rather a means of character development. Both men understood that the wild places of the nation were essential to the human experience, and both also understood that those wild places were disappearing. Developing a strategy to preserve them, however, posed a fundamental question: Were humans supposed to receive passively what nature had to give, or were they to take it? Muir and the Sierra Club believed that "received" was the answer and that the invisible spiritual gifts nature provided were enough reason to preserve it. Roosevelt and the Boone and Crockett Club, on the other hand, believed that "taken" was the answer, that there were physical trophies to be won in the wilderness. Put in simpler terms, Muir stressed preservation of the wilderness, leaving it as unaltered by humans as possible; Roosevelt was more prone to stress conservation of the wilderness, that is, managing its resources in a way that humans would gain.

During his first term of office Roosevelt signed the National Reclamation Act, more often called the Newlands Reclamation Act after Representative Francis G. Newlands of Nevada, who introduced the bill in Congress. Conservation was a rather sticky matter for Roosevelt and the Republicans. Theirs was the party of the Homestead Act, which allowed individuals to claim designated public lands for private family farms. The Newlands Reclamation Act was designed to build large dams and subsequent irrigation projects that would ultimately turn land unfarmable by Euro-American methods into farmland. Private enterprise had failed to accomplish this. Open competition for water rights had resulted only in dams built farther and farther upstream and monopolization of the water. The federal government was the only entity capable of systematically building the large dams necessary for regulating rivers that flowed between states. Those dams had to be paid for, and it seemed only fair that the people directly benefitting from them should do that. The federal government maintained intermediary ownership of the dams and the regulated water, which it sold to water users' associations made up of farmers who were allowed to divert their fair share of the water. The plan verged on being socialistic except that the water users' associations would eventually gain autonomy over the water by paying off the cost of the irrigation projects.

In the face of criticism over such massive federal involvement, Roosevelt liked to point out that the federal government routinely improved harbors and dredged rivers for commercial purposes without arousing complaints. Newlands-style reclamation would be more of the same, except that deserts would be involved. But that terrain is important to understanding Roosevelt's type of conservation: there was no intention to preserve the desert landscape. The intention was to completely alter the landscape so that agriculture could flourish. Ultimately these irrigation projects were successful, probably more so than Roosevelt or Newlands could have imagined, spawning not only farms but feeding the region's growing need for electricity and supporting the growth of cities. Phoenix, Arizona, an affluent city of 1.5 million people, for instance, depends on electricity generated by dams on the Salt River that were built by the federal government. The Roosevelt Dam was the first such dam constructed under the Newlands program, and Theodore Roosevelt proudly attended its dedication ceremony in 1911.

Roosevelt attributed much of his reputation as a conservationist president to his friend and adviser Gifford Pinchot, a fellow member of the Boone and Crockett Club. Pinchot was a Yale graduate who had gone to Europe to study forestry, there being few formal training centers in the United States at the time. Pinchot, like Roosevelt, saw nature as something from which physical gifts could be taken—for profit as well as for personal enjoyment. When Pinchot became the nation's first chief forester in 1905, he was made head of the U.S. Forestry Service—which had been moved from the Department of the Interior to the Department of Agriculture. John Muir liked Roosevelt well enough to enjoy camping with him, but he could not abide Pinchot. It wasn't that Pinchot was unlikeable, but his belief that the nation should manage its natural reserves through projects such as Newlands' reclamation was diametrically opposed to Muir's own philosophy. In fact, Pinchot's beliefs coincided with those of his day. In essence, Pinchot saw the nation's forests as tree farms. If harvested, a forest needed replanting, but it was there to be used.

Roosevelt and Pinchot made a formidable team. President Roosevelt used the 1891 Forest Reserve Act to great effect, turning nearly 150 million acres of forestland into national forests, which Pinchot then managed. The national forests could certainly be used for recreation, and even for Muir-style spiritualism, but entrepreneurs could also lease the lands for grazing and timber. Roosevelt supported this system as long as the lands were fairly administered. And it did halt wholesale demolition of the nation's forests at a time when railroad ties needed to be changed out every three years and thousands of acres of trees were being cleared each year. Roosevelt's administration also removed from sale more than 80 million acres of land deemed mineral rich.

There are a variety of ways to look at the early-twentieth-century conservation movement. Certainly it helped to preserve intact large areas of natural lands for future generations, but—again to stress the point—they were for Americans to use. This use might be recreational or commercial or even for national defense (e.g., coal and timber), but however the lands were used, America's natural resources would be doled out by federal bureaucracies. As to commercial usage, much of the protected lands were in the West, although many of the business concerns that wanted access to their resources were based in the East. The conservation movement was thus much more popular in the East than in the West, and undoubtedly it helped maintain the West as a colonial economy. Indeed, it was from the West that protests came most loudly, and it was congressional leaders from that region who were most active in repealing, in 1907, the Forest Reserve Act that had underpinned most of Roosevelt's conservation programs. But Roosevelt used the act until the last moment, creating twenty-one new forest reserves before the repeal came into effect. It was the sort of ploy that Roosevelt could get away with, but the conservation movement needed his popularity and energy behind it. In 1908, his last full year in office, Roosevelt created the National Conservation Commission with the help of several state governors. At the head of the commission he placed Gifford Pinchot, who set off from Washington to take inventory of the nation's natural resources. Despite the three-volume report Pinchot produced, Congress refused further funding of the commission, and Roosevelt was no longer in the White House to protect it. Gifford Pinchot's job did not survive the Taft administration.

Roosevelt, Pinchot, and Muir disagreed on many points, but the one on which all could agree was that the federal government needed to take a larger stance in governing the natural environment. To that end Roosevelt was quite successful. The conservation movement as Roosevelt and Pinchot saw it was also quite successful; nature was being managed in such a way that its gifts could be taken, and even inventoried. Although some environmentalists then and today would disagree with Roosevelt's philosophy of managing resources for the service of humans, Roosevelt had done more than any other president to date to shape the American outdoors as we know them.

Roosevelt was proud of his accomplishments as a conservationist, and they are well remembered today, but during his own time he was better known as "the trustbuster"—"trust" referring to a business model in which competing businesses were acquired and combined to reduce competition and to support price stability. For the most part, trusts were an understandable response to a volatile economy. The United States was rapidly industrializing, and had been for half a century by the time Roosevelt became president. The root of the problem lay in the fact that industrialization made production much more efficient. Efficient production, in turn, could easily put too many goods of a certain type on the market, leading to a precipitous drop in the product's wholesale price. When this happened on a large scale, workers were fired, markets shrank even further, and "panics" occurred—essentially what would be called recessions today. In order to avoid these panics, a large-scale owner in a specific industry would acquire control of as much of the industry as possible in order to limit production and competition, and consequently be able to set prices. The Parker Brothers game "Monopoly" is based on this business model.

This would seem to be fairly straightforward capitalism with essentially self-regulating industries. But the problem was that the industries did not regulate themselves for the general good, but rather for their owners' good by keeping prices high, keeping wages low, and preventing new businesses from entering the industry; in short, trusts deterred free-market capitalism. Congress had moved to regulate trust-building in 1890 by passing the Sherman Antitrust Act, which regarded trusts as being contractually designed to restrain trade, and therefore illegal and subject to government dissolution. But the Sherman Antitrust Act did little to halt the growth of trusts—in part, at least, because the act did not provide a solid definition of what a trust was. For instance, the Supreme Court decided on four occasions that a labor union could exist in restraint of trade and therefore operate illegally. The Supreme Court also decided that there was a marked difference between restraint of trade in manufacturing and in commerce, and that Sherman applied only to commerce.

The Republican Party was beginning to distinguish itself as the pro-business party (a change from its roots as the free-labor party), especially under McKinley, and while Roosevelt did not always follow the party line, he was certainly not against business. The nation was thus taken by surprise when, in 1902, President Roosevelt leveled an attack on four of the wealthiest businessmen in America, including J. P. Morgan and John D. Rockefeller, who had formed a railroad trust known as the Northern Securities Company. Also surprising was Roosevelt's use of the Sherman Antitrust Act in the case, a use the Supreme Court upheld a couple of years later, deeming a railroad trust to be in restraint of commerce. Later in 1902 Roosevelt struck again, this time against Chicago's "meat trust." Interestingly, during his time as a Rough Rider Roosevelt had complained about the "horrible stuff called 'canned fresh beef,'" so he may have had a personal "beef" against the industry. If so, he got his revenge when the Supreme Court again upheld his use of the Sherman

Antitrust Act. These antitrust actions did not attempt to destroy the companies themselves; the names Morgan, Rockefeller, and Swift and Company (chiefly named in the meat trust suit) remain important in the U.S. business world. Instead, Roosevelt seems to have been firing a warning shot over the trust-builders' bow.

But why open fire at all? The postwar economy was going strong, and public opinion was not especially desirous of the attack; and the advantage of being the pro-business party is that your party has businesses backing its campaign treasuries. In all, there seems to have been more risk than potential reward for Roosevelt. Historians have offered a variety of explanations. For instance, Roosevelt had a deep-rooted sense of morality and fair play, which led him to be more aggressive than his predecessors in stamping out obvious transgressions in the economy. Another classic interpretation is that Roosevelt, alongside other reformers of the Progressive Era, was suffering from status anxiety. In this interpretation, the natural aristocracy was being threatened by the nouveau riche corporate oligarchy, and the threat was so profound that some members of the natural aristocracy had to descend into the world of politics to fight for their social class. This argument has the benefit of classical support going back to Aristotle, who considered aristocracy and oligarchy natural enemies. Or perhaps Roosevelt and other members of his generation were seeking economic and political reforms because they were influenced by modern science and engineering to seek order in all facets of public life and institutions, and were encouraged by similar reform movements in European nations. They thought in terms of systems, and so created them in an attempt to obtain the order they sought. A number of Roosevelt's reforms could be cited to support this argument, including the 1903 creation of the U.S. Department of Labor and Commerce, which included the Bureau of Corporations, to give the federal government some leverage and additional regulatory power in the economy. (Big Business had led to Big Labor, which had set off social strife because the two are naturally antagonistic forces. Big Government was necessary to balance the equation; that is, Big Business plus Big Labor equals Big Government.) We thus have the divergent but overlapping ideas that Roosevelt's trust-busting was based on his personal sense of morality, that as a member of his class and generation he was motivated by fear that the natural aristocracy was giving way to the nouveau riche, and that he was searching for an orderly process to solve a variety of problems; or perhaps some combination of these.

A more cynical view of his trust-busting would portray Roosevelt as a politically savvy man who was already courting public opinion for the elections of 1904. The fact that Roosevelt was indeed elected by a wide margin in 1904 supports this view. Less obvious is the fact that 70 percent of the Republicans' campaign funds came from corporations. This could be seen as an attempt to pay off the umpire, but a more realistic interpretation would have it that knowing there was an umpire, and knowing that the umpire was attempting to maintain the rules, promised the stability that Big Business had been seeking all along.

Big Labor, too, found Roosevelt to its liking. The president had personally intervened as arbitrator in a coal miners' strike in the winter of 1902–3—no coal meant no heat, making it an important national issue. When mine owners refused to discuss that issue, Roosevelt threatened to federalize the mines and have soldiers work the coal. The mine owners agreed to wage increases. Prior presidents had used their command of the military in different ways and usually in support of property owners (a worker protesting working conditions could be shot if he or she interrupted the mail, for example), so Roosevelt's tactic signaled a refreshing change. His handling of the coal strike reflected his international diplomacy—the message in both cases was that instability could result in the employment of force, but he was willing to discuss the issue.

Historians have pointed out that Roosevelt's image as a trustbuster was overblown. His real intention was not to destroy monopolistic corporations but to regulate them so that they played fair. And in that, Roosevelt was being consistent. Larger corporations were more capable of competing internationally, so his view of corporate America aligned with his view of global America. The Panama Canal was not built for military purposes alone, after all. So long as he remained popular with public opinion, he remained a force with whom it was better to bargain than to fight. And bargaining was something Roosevelt did very well. A few examples will illustrate his skills.

Railroads at the time were the single most important industry in the United States. Creating railroads seems to have been something of a fad in the late 1800s; hundreds of minor lines were built throughout the country. Over time, most of these small lines had become incorporated into larger systems, with "incorporation" being a polite term for a variety of acquisition methods ranging from cash disbursements to violence. These larger systems now controlled the railroads, which brought some uniformity to them, but irregularities remained, particularly in price fixing. Farmers, for instance, complained that they were being gouged by railroads while major corporations that could afford to pay more were receiving lower rates provided in the form of kickbacks or rebates. Pricing could vary wildly according to the state, the time of year, and any number of other variables. The railroads themselves were against the kickback system, and it was they who approached the federal government to pass laws regulating rebates. That law, the Elkins Act, which passed during Roosevelt's first term, required railroads to post rates and not deviate from them. This did not solve the pricing problem from the consumer standpoint, however, and Roosevelt pushed Congress for additional legislation—bucking some fellow Republicans in the process. Congress responded with the Hepburn Act of 1906, which increased the power of the Interstate Commerce Commission so that it could establish maximum rates and require the railroad companies to standardize their accounting systems so that noncompliance would be more obvious. In this instance, the railroads had initiated federal intervention, Congress had passed the necessary laws, but Roosevelt, in the eyes of public opinion, was the hero.

Newspapers were the most influential factor in the formation of public opinion in the early twentieth century, but literature had a great deal to do with it as well. Railroads got their send-up in Frank Norris' novel *The Octopus* (1901), which exposed the rampant violence brought on by railroad consolidation. It is less clear which aspect of Upton Sinclair's *The Jungle* (1906) caused the greater uproar—the immigrant hero's turn to socialism or the depiction of working conditions in Chicago's meatpacking factories—but eating a sausage while reading the novel requires a strong stomach. After the book's publication, members of the Armour family, Chicago's largest meatpackers, pointed out that the Armour Company's livestock was government inspected and then, to improve public opinion, called for even more inspection. Congress responded with the 1906 Meat Inspection Act, which called for inspection not only of the animals but of factory cleanliness as well (score another victory over this "horrible stuff called 'canned fresh beef'"). Roosevelt signed a second consumer protection act into law on the same day he signed the Meat Inspection

Act. The Pure Food and Drug Act, which called for accurate labels on drugs and food, was initiated by pharmaceutical companies. In this case, too, an industry had sought regulation, Congress had provided it, and Roosevelt came out as public opinion's hero.

As government regulations mounted, some business leaders and shareholders began to fear Roosevelt, especially after John D. Rockefeller claimed that the president's trust-busting was undermining the economy. The stock market did in fact take a downturn in the spring of 1907—although it was more a product of overspeculation and excessive credit than Roosevelt's reforms. Roosevelt believed the panic on Wall Street was simply a typical market correction, but when businesses began to fail that summer he began using treasury funds to stabilize at-risk banks. Even while he worked closely with J. P. Morgan to save the finance industry from its own excesses, criticism was coming at him from all quarters. Late in the fall of 1907, Morgan hatched a plan for his U.S. Steel to purchase the stock of Moore and Schley, an at-risk brokerage firm. Normally, Morgan purchasing stock would not have been a big issue, but Moore and Schley was heavily invested in Tennessee Coal and Iron, which happened to be U.S. Steel's biggest rival. Morgan, via assistants, assured Roosevelt that the purchase was intended only to save Moore and Schley, bring some confidence back to Wall Street, and hurry the end of the panic, and Roosevelt agreed to allow the purchase without antitrust prosecution. The deal did help eliminate some of the panic, although the $150 million in treasury bonds doled out by the Roosevelt administration was probably more important in that regard. The Panic of 1907 left a bad taste in Roosevelt's mouth, and he eventually came to believe that one of its causes was the attempt by greedy business interests to discredit his policies.

Since taking office in 1901 Roosevelt had largely continued to pursue McKinley's policies, as he had pledged to do. His administration had expanded and modernized national defense, had taken an active and often internationally applauded role in diplomatic affairs, and had developed infrastructures for governing the environment and for stabilizing labor relations, and he had expanded the possibilities of commerce in all these areas. He had entered office generally believing that business was akin to a sport, and may the best man win. "In the last analysis it is the thrift, energy, self-mastery, and business intelligence of each man which have most to do with deciding whether he rises or falls,"

Roosevelt wrote in 1900, adding that "the best scheme of government can do little more than provide against injustice, and then let the individual rise or fall on his own merits."[10] But he had also been raised to believe that having money meant having social responsibilities and moral obligations. During the Panic of 1907 he saw simple greed for more money combine with ingratitude for his work. It was a turning point in his thinking and led him afterward to write: "It is better for the government to help a poor man to make a living for his family than to help a rich man make more profit for his company."[11] In a way, his own trust—in the virtues of wealth—had been busted.

Abraham Lincoln surrounded himself with a team of his political rivals, men whose ambition sometimes influenced their counsel and decisions. Roosevelt, on the other hand, created a team of capable administrators who were less well known than Lincoln's cabinet of presidential hopefuls but who ultimately proved effective and trustworthy. Roosevelt depended particularly on Elihu Root and Gifford Pinchot, but when it came time to choose a successor in 1908, it was William Howard Taft he selected. Taft had executive experience gained as governor of the Philippines, had served well as secretary of war, and had been trained in the law and had served as a federal judge.

The fact that Roosevelt was "choosing a successor" gives some indication of how popular he had become. But party support for his choice was no foregone conclusion. During Roosevelt's presidency the Republican Party had split into two factions: the Roosevelt Republicans and the Stand Pat Republicans. Among the leaders of the Stand Patters was Senator Nelson Aldrich, who was said to be on the payroll of Rockefeller, Morgan, or both (depending on which rumor one chose to believe), and who was pushing Republicans to nominate Senator Charles Fairbanks. Other potential frontrunners included Elihu Root, whom many dismissed as unelectable because of his corporate ties, and Governor Charles Evans Hughes of New York. Going into the Republican convention there were three major possibilities for the nomination: Taft, Fairbanks, and Roosevelt, who had in 1904 pledged not to run for president in 1908, but whom some expected to accept the nomination if enough groundswell support emerged. Even some Republicans who typically disagreed with

Roosevelt's choices supported Taft, thinking that in nominating Taft they were preventing Roosevelt's possible nomination.

The result was that William Howard Taft, who had never been elected to any public office in his career and never would be again, became the most recent Republican to have the honor of defeating William Jennings Bryan in a presidential election. His platform was Rooseveltian: conservation and more trust-busting, but also a lower tariff, reflecting a marked shift in the Republican Party from the days of McKinley. But while Taft followed Roosevelt, he did not have Roosevelt's personality or his ability to handle the press, manage public opinion, or arbitrate his way to the top of a balance of power. He was not a bad president, but more important, he was not a good politician. Taft's shortcomings in this area were furthered by the civil war going on within the Republican Party. The Roosevelt Republicans were led by Senator Robert "Fightin' Bob" La Follette, a Wisconsinite who thought Roosevelt had not gone nearly far enough with his reforms. La Follette and his Insurgents (Fightin' Bob did not like being called a Roosevelt Republican) were facing off against the Stand Patters, and Taft could not hold them together. Indeed, he could not hold himself in the middle and began drifting right, toward the Stand Patters.

Theodore Roosevelt, meanwhile, was having a great time being a former president. He was able to combine several of his passions into one trip to Africa, where he hunted big game (his trophies included a rhinoceros and a hippopotamus) with one of his sons while working with scientists and taxidermists who prepared the collected animals for the Smithsonian's collection and writing about his adventures. In 1910 he and his wife toured Europe, meeting several heads of state (Roosevelt was not completely unimpressed) during the trip. He addressed the Nobel Prize Committee, lectured at major universities, and generally held forth on public occasions. His popularity in the United States was of the sort we would call "celebrity," and so the media kept Americans abreast of his travels and adventures. And then, in the summer of 1910, he returned home.

Roosevelt seems to have genuinely believed that President Taft would continue the Roosevelt administration's policies. It was not that Roosevelt was naïve, but rather that he had a great deal of confidence in his policies and thought of Taft as a capable administrator of them. But

Taft was diverging from the program. He took three major actions that indicated he had struck out in his own direction. The first of these was his support of the Payne-Aldrich Tariff, which made the average import duty about 27 percent less than the Dingley Tariff that had been passed during President McKinley's administration. Although the average duty on imports fell, it did so only because tariffs on some items, such as timber, were reduced. La Follette and the Insurgents fought hard to prevent the lower tariff, seeking across-the-board cuts, but the Stand Patters in the Senate made sure that big industries, especially steel and iron, remained heavily protected, and they used some dubious maneuvers to keep the bill from being fully examined and debated. Taft had promised La Follette that he would veto Payne-Aldrich when it reached him, but instead he signed it and then went on to publicly declare it the best tariff ever. The Insurgents felt thoroughly betrayed.

Roosevelt was more personally affected when President Taft fired his good friend Gifford Pinchot from his post as chief of the U.S. Forest Service. Indeed, some sort of discipline was probably warranted because Pinchot had publicly accused Secretary of the Interior Richard Ballinger of favoring monopolistic corporations when leasing Alaskan coal lands. The Ballinger-Pinchot Affair was quite a scandal, with Pinchot losing his position after he sent a letter to an Insurgent senator who read it into the Senate Record. Ultimately a congressional investigation found that Ballinger's actions were within the rules, but public opinion was against him and he resigned to protect Taft.

Completing the rift between Roosevelt and Taft was the Taft administration's decision to prosecute U.S. Steel for violating antitrust laws in its acquisition of Tennessee Coal and Iron via the Moore and Schley buyout. The tariff issue had raised the Insurgents' ire at Taft, and the Ballinger-Pinchot Affair had angered both the Insurgents and Roosevelt, but the U.S. Steel antitrust suit was a personal insult. He and Morgan had agreed to a deal that exempted the latter from prosecution under antitrust laws, with Roosevelt hoping that he was halting the Panic of 1907. In fact, Morgan put one over on him, and within a couple of years everyone knew it. La Follette had been quick to point out the similarities between the Northern Securities case and Tennessee Coal and Iron at the time, but Roosevelt had cut the deal anyway. Taft's decision to prosecute made Roosevelt look foolish. And that was something he could not brook.

As Taft was moving toward the Stand Patters, Roosevelt was moving toward the Insurgents. The fact that he was moving at all seemed irrelevant to some people, who thought of him in that way the nation thinks of a former president—as someone whose presence makes events seem more important. But Roosevelt got sucked back into the fray almost immediately after his return to the United States in the summer of 1910, lured in by New York Republicans who wanted him to pull some strings to get a bill passed. When Roosevelt went to Osawatomie, Kansas, to address a crowd commemorating John Brown, his relevance quickly became clear. He began by talking about the Civil War and President Lincoln, but by the time he ended, the speech was all about Theodore Roosevelt and the New Nationalism.

The New Nationalism might seem an old idea to modern readers—in fact, President Barack Obama gave a speech in Osawatomie in 2011 that cited Roosevelt's New Nationalism as a model for today's political economy. But it certainly turned some heads when Roosevelt first laid it out. The gist of the idea was that the federal government, with a fully empowered executive branch, needed to take a strong regulatory stance in the national economy. The piecemeal legislation enacted by local and state governments was no longer sufficient to protect the people from profit-mongering corporations. Furthermore, the people needed the additional democratic protections that a national income tax, direct election of senators, and a judiciary empowered to contemplate social as well as legal justice would give them. Workers needed safe working conditions, worker's compensation programs, a minimum wage, and maximum hours.

Practiced observers were quick to understand what Roosevelt's speech meant. Two months after Roosevelt laid out the components of the New Nationalism, former senator Joseph Foraker, who had stood up to Roosevelt during the Brownsville affair, noted that "they are set forth in the nature of a platform for a new party." Foraker's assessment was right on the mark, but he ventured to be even more accurate: "Possibly they are intended for that use only in the event that the distinguished author [Roosevelt] be not nominated for the Presidency by either of the old parties."[12]

Late in 1911, just as Foraker had predicted, Roosevelt began letting Republicans know that he was available for the 1912 nomination. In

February 1912, however, Roosevelt made a tactical error by expanding the New Nationalism plank to include the recall of judicial decisions—in essence giving voters the ability to overturn court judgments. Regardless of the desirability of overturning specific decisions, the Constitution provides for an independent judiciary in the hope that justice will be done through a deliberative magisterial process, not according to what is popular at the moment. Stand Patters, who had been charging Roosevelt with constitutional transgressions for some time, finally had proof that Roosevelt was a dangerous radical. In the Republican convention that summer, Stand Patters were able to hold off the Roosevelt delegates and renominate President Taft. In response, Roosevelt's supporters insisted that he run on a separate ticket, which he did. On August 5 the Progressive Party, formed by Fightin' Bob La Follette in 1911 but relatively obscure until Roosevelt grasped it as a vehicle, met in convention in Chicago and nominated Theodore Roosevelt as its candidate.

The Progressive Party soon acquired a nickname. After Roosevelt pronounced himself as fit as a bull moose, the Progressives were tagged the "Bull Moose Party." And like a real bull moose, he had no chance of becoming president in 1912. A mere three months remained before Election Day, and the nascent party did not have the campaign apparatus to compete with the Democrats and Republicans. But Roosevelt made a strong showing nevertheless. Having declared himself a man of the people, he appealed to the people's emotions if not their reason. On accepting the nomination, for instance, he closed his speech by thundering, "We stand at Armageddon, and we battle for the Lord."[13] The battle was the important thing, not the victory, Roosevelt told his followers. At one point in the campaign Roosevelt was shot in the chest by a would-be assassin but went on and gave a lengthy speech as blood oozed through his vest.

Americans love drama in their politics and Roosevelt provided that, but the election came down to the issues. The big one for voters was between Roosevelt's New Nationalism and Democratic nominee Woodrow Wilson's New Freedom. In many ways the two programs were very similar, but they differed on one major point: New Nationalism accepted that corporations would combine into large trusts and deemed such combinations acceptable as long as the trusts were sufficiently regulated by government (Big Business needs Big Government); New Freedom denied the validity of trusts and argued that government should continue to prosecute them while fostering a competitive market that welcomed small business owners and reduced federal regulation (Small Business needs Protective Government). Voters also considered the Taft platform, which focused on less spectacular economic reforms, and the Socialist platform, which called for very spectacular economic reforms, including the nationalization of the interstate transportation and banking industries.

There were no exit polls to indicate what voters were thinking, but the election results speak for themselves. Voters decisively chose the Democrat Woodrow Wilson and New Freedom. Wilson received 435 electoral votes; Roosevelt carried 6 states and won 88 electoral votes; and Taft finished third with 2 states and 8 electoral votes. Wilson won the popular vote by a wide margin as well, but that might not have been the case if the Republicans had not split. The combined Roosevelt-Taft vote was about 7.5 million to Wilson's 6.2 million (Eugene Debs pulled in nearly 900,000 for the Socialist Party). For the first time since his 1886 New York City mayoral campaign, Roosevelt had failed to win an election. But there would be no comeback after 1912. Wilson had won the presidency, and Taft had won the Republican Party. Roosevelt finished second to Wilson, but second place had the same result for Roosevelt as fourth place had for Eugene Debs.

The "Bull Moose bolt" pulled the Progressives out of the Republican Party, and many of them saw no need to return. Wilson was working toward many of the reforms they wanted, and many Bull Moosers went on to join the Democrats; others stuck with the Progressive Party until the 1920s. Roosevelt returned to the Republican Party during the 1916 elections, but with the exception of a few remaining westerners, the party's progressive wing was essentially destroyed. The Stand Patters had won, ensuring that the Republican Party would become the nation's conservative party.

When Thomas Platt pushed Roosevelt out of New York in 1900 in order to save his Republican machine, he unwittingly helped create one of the most popular and interesting presidents in the history of the United States. In one form or another, Roosevelt dominated U.S. politics for nearly a dozen years and influenced domestic and global politics for longer than that. But on November 6, 1912, the Roosevelt Era concluded—at least for Theodore Roosevelt.

Conclusion

Losing the election in 1912 did not lower Roosevelt's spirits overmuch. He had taken blows before; after all, he was a man who boxed for recreation. After taking his version of a break for several months—during which he wrote his autobiography, a classic of the genre—he set off on another adventure, this time to South America. There he hunted and explored the river that is now named for him: the Río Roosevelt. This particular adventure was more harrowing than his usual affair and almost resulted in his death deep in an Amazonian jungle after he became ill. He never wholly recovered from that illness.

After he emerged from the jungle, nearly sixty pounds lighter, Roosevelt returned to the United States to deal with the 1914 midterm elections, providing endorsements to some candidates and using his prestige against others. But political campaigns became overshadowed in August when a Bosnian assassin killed the heir to the Austro-Hungarian crown. Austria-Hungary declared war on Serbia, Russia declared war on Austria-Hungary, and Germany declared war on Russia and France and invaded neutral Belgium, bringing Great Britain into the fray. The Great War was on, and the question in the United States was what to do about it. For Roosevelt, the only possible answer was, "Hasten forward quickly there!" to prepare the nation for war. But President Wilson sought to keep America neutral.

The Great War absorbed Roosevelt for the remainder of his life. He feared that the United States was unprepared for self-defense, much less for war. He wanted America to support France and Great Britain because a victorious Germany would pose the greater threat to the United States—not to the mainland but to its island possessions and its general authority in the Western Hemisphere. He became a major voice of the preparedness movement, and although he did not join any of the organizations associated with that movement, his influence aided their cause. Roosevelt argued that there were benefits to enlarging the armed forces and beginning to train men for battle. The nation would be less vulnerable to attack if it was prepared for war, but he also felt that the experience of being in the military would create better Americans. At the time, a significant percentage of the nation's population consisted of immigrants, many of whom maintained strong ties to their European homelands. Roosevelt thought that serving the United States would help to break down ethnic boundaries and hasten Americanization. Various preparedness groups, often with impressive financial backing, served as lobbyists and were able to help sway Congress to initiate some preparedness measures in the summer of 1916.

In 1916 President Wilson ran for reelection under the slogan "He kept us out of war" (a slogan Wilson did not like). By that time, Roosevelt was convinced that Wilson was a coward. When the Progressive Party nominated Roosevelt as its presidential candidate, though, he refused the nomination—he would run again, he said, only if the Republican Party nominated him as well. The Republicans chose Charles Evans Hughes instead. The Progressive Party was no longer a real factor in American politics, and Roosevelt returned to the Republican Party, which was glad to have him back now that he was more clearly in opposition to the Democrats. Hughes nearly defeated the incumbent Wilson. Had two thousand Californians voted differently, President Hughes would have taken office. But it was Wilson who addressed Congress and asked for a declaration of war against Germany less than a month after his second inauguration.

If the United States was going to war, Theodore Roosevelt was determined to go too, and he met with Wilson to ask for a command. As the nation's former commander in chief, he argued, he was owed an appointment, and he wanted to command a division of 25,000 troops. President Wilson apparently did not completely dash his hopes; he left that to Secretary of War Newton D. Baker. Wilson and Baker were patient and polite as Roosevelt continued to hound them, but they remained unmoved, and Roosevelt had no backing from the general staff for the appointment. The other Allies voiced approval of a Roosevelt Division, but they would have taken anyone at that point; the Great War was a meat grinder, and Europe was running out of bodies with which to feed it.

In truth, Roosevelt was in no shape to command troops in battle. He was in his late fifties, and the sickness that had nearly killed him in the jungle continued to come back from time to time. Few people knew that he was blind in one eye. Roosevelt complained that politics was behind Wilson's refusal to give him a command, that he was being punished for criticizing Wilson, but it was just as likely that Wilson saw no military benefit in the plan—or perhaps he was simply too humane to send Roosevelt over the top. Even William Howard Taft felt bad for Roosevelt, saying that regardless of any grudge he might hold, "I certainly could wish him no worse luck than to be sick in bed while Woodrow runs his war."[1]

While his four sons were fighting in Europe, Roosevelt fought on the home front. His fight against the Germans began to include German Americans, who were already battling accusations of anti-Americanism. Roosevelt continued to write and give public appearances as his health declined. In 1918 he lost the hearing in one ear. On the day the war finally ended, November 11, 1918, Roosevelt was in the hospital being diagnosed with "inflammatory rheumatism." He returned home but continued to weaken. On January 5, 1919, he wrote one last editorial and then went to bed. He did not awaken. Before dawn on January 6 a blood clot stopped his heart.

The Rough Riders were among those who attended the funeral of Theodore Roosevelt. No formal eulogy was given, but Vice President Thomas Marshall's remark sums up the essence of the man: "Death had to take him sleeping, for if Roosevelt had been awake, there would have been a fight."[2]

Born just prior to the beginning of one war, Theodore Roosevelt died just after another ended. Although he fought in neither of those wars, in important ways fighting defined him. From his childhood encounter with bullies that turned a puny boy into a boxer, to the hard-won cowboy skills he turned into cavalry prowess, to his ferocity in political battles, Roosevelt was always a fighter. And yet to consider him merely in that light would be gross oversimplification. His battles, at least as an adult, arose from his staunch patriotism.

Roosevelt believed that war fostered manly virtues, and he was eager to participate in the conflicts that affected the United States, but as a way to advance America's goals. The impressive feat of diplomacy that gained him the Nobel Peace Prize can also be viewed as an effort to defend America's interests in the Pacific. Likewise, the $40,000 prize money he gave to the National Civic Federation, an organization created to foster communication between business and labor leaders and improve the possibility of "industrial peace," was given in defense of America's economy. "In the present state of the world's development industrial peace is even more essential than international peace," Roosevelt wrote in his autobiography.[3]

War with other nations was one thing, and could even be a good thing, but Americans fighting amongst themselves over money was not good. Roosevelt's identity as a Progressive was based on his belief that the vast disparities of wealth that divided Americans had to be in some way alleviated to give all Americans the rights promised by the Constitution. That particular war was not one that even Theodore Roosevelt could win.

During the course of his lifetime Roosevelt's perceptions of wealth changed, as did those of Americans in general. "I was of course while in college taught the *laissez-faire* doctrines—one of them being free trade— then accepted as canonical," Roosevelt wrote in his autobiography. "But there was almost no teaching of the need for collective action, and of the fact that in addition to, not as a substitute for, individual responsibility, there is a collective responsibility."[4] That collective responsibility, he came to believe, was best undertaken through government action at the federal level. Twenty years after Theodore Roosevelt and New Nationalism lost the elections of 1912, another Roosevelt won an election. That victory was a signal that most Americans had generally come to accept the need for expansive federal regulation of the economy. But Franklin Roosevelt's New Deal and greater fame should not overshadow Theodore Roosevelt's many accomplishments.

Theodore Roosevelt's leadership qualities, reforms, and larger-than-life persona brought national politics to the forefront of Americans' lives. During his era, machine politicians began to give way to skilled career experts. "Bureaucrat" is often considered a derisive term, but there could be no equality of representation as long as good-old-boy networks controlled the government. Even the military, one of the last bastions of that system, came to value and rely on experts after Roosevelt helped modernize the Army and popularize the Navy. Franklin Roosevelt's actions and policies helped to sculpt America as a world power, but Theodore Roosevelt was responsible for expanding the nation's influence abroad.

Roosevelt did not do any of this alone, of course, although his energy in supporting the causes he valued was so extraordinary that he sometimes seems to have done so. He was simply overwhelming in some ways. "It was hard to tell him anything," famed muckraker Lincoln Steffens wrote of Roosevelt. "It was easy to make him talk, even about a State secret, but to reverse the process and make him listen was well-nigh impossible." Steffens learned that there were a few minutes every day during which Roosevelt was quiet—when his valet was shaving him with a straight razor—and took advantage of that time to discuss social concerns. At one point Steffens told Roosevelt his theory that Roosevelt did not so much make up his mind about issues as "mull them over somewhere else in your nervous system and—and form your conclusion in, say, your hips." After considering the point, Roosevelt concurred. "Do you know, that's true. I do think down—down there somewhere."[5] Roosevelt's "down there" thinking led to massive federal investment in the military and in the environment. It also shaped, however inadvertently, the Republican Party as the nation's conservative political party. Whether or not he was a leader of the progressive reform movement may be debated, but it is very difficult to write a book about the progressive movement that does not in some way mention Theodore Roosevelt, the most famous American of his generation at home and abroad.

Notes

CHAPTER 1 Learning the Ropes

1. Among the most famous Progressives born during the Civil War era were Jane Addams (Illinois, 1860), William Borah (Illinois, 1865), Louis Brandeis (Kentucky, 1856), William Jennings Bryan (Illinois, 1860), Eugene Debs (Indiana, 1865), John Dewey (Vermont, 1859), W. E. B. DuBois (Massachusetts, 1868), Charles Evans Hughes (New York, 1862), Florence Kelley (Pennsylvania, 1859), Walter Rauschenbusch (New York, 1861), William Howard Taft (Ohio, 1857), Lillian Wald (Ohio, 1867), and Woodrow Wilson (Virginia, 1856).
2. Theodore Roosevelt, *Theodore Roosevelt, an Autobiography* (1913; New York: Da Capo Press, 1985), 25.
3. Chauncey M. Depew, *My Memories of Eighty Years* (New York: Charles Scribner's Sons, 1924), 159.
4. Quoted in Mark Wahlgren Summers, *The Gilded Age, or The Hazard of New Functions* (Upper Saddle River, N.J.: Prentice-Hall, 1997), 210.
5. Owen Wister, *Roosevelt: The Story of a Friendship* (New York: Macmillan, 1930), 27.
6. Ibid.
7. Theodore Roosevelt, *Hunting the Grisly and Other Sketches* (1889; New York: Barnes and Noble Books, 2003), 29, 45.
8. Book review: "Roosevelt's *Hunting Trips of a Ranchman*," *Atlantic Monthly* 336 (October 1885): 563–64.
9. Book review: "Roosevelt's *Winning of the West*," *Atlantic Monthly* 385 (November 1889): 694.
10. Frederick Jackson Turner, "*The Winning of the West*, by Theodore Roosevelt," *American Historical Review* 2 (October 1896): 175.
11. Henry Steele Commager, *The American Mind: An Interpretation of American Thought and Character since the 1880s* (New Haven: Yale University Press, 1950), 348.
12. Roosevelt, *Autobiography*, 96.
13. Theodore Roosevelt, "The College Graduate and Public Life," *Atlantic Monthly* 442 (August 1894): 255, 256.
14. Jacob A. Riis, *The Making of an American* (New York: Macmillan, 1902), 325.

CHAPTER 2 Charging the Army
1. Roosevelt, *Autobiography*, 218.
2. Ibid., 222.
3. Theodore Roosevelt, *The Rough Riders* (1899; New York: Barnes and Noble Books, 2004), 35.

CHAPTER 3 Taking Up the White House Burden
1. Depew, *My Memories of Eighty Years*, 161–62.
2. Ibid., 169–71.
3. Wister, *Story of a Friendship*, 92–94.
4. Roosevelt, *Autobiography*, 568.
5. Ibid., 564.
6. Ibid., 564–65.
7. Theodore Roosevelt, *The Strenuous Life: Essays and Addresses* (New York: Century, 1901), 37.
8. As quoted in Lewis L. Gould, *The Presidency of Theodore Roosevelt* (Lawrence: University Press of Kansas, 1991), 239.
9. Richard White, *"It's Your Misfortune and None of My Own": A New History of the American West* (Norman: University of Oklahoma Press, 1991), 410.
10. Ibid., 148.
11. Roosevelt, *Autobiography*, 417.
12. Foraker delivered his speech on October 22, 1910, in Marysville, Ohio; it is reproduced in Joseph B. Foraker, *Notes of a Busy Life*, 3rd ed., vol. 2 (Cincinnati: Stewart and Kidd, 1917), 433.
13. Quoted in a variety of sources, including William H. Harbaugh, *The Life and Times of Theodore Roosevelt*, rev. ed. (New York: Oxford University Press, 1975), 416.

Conclusion
1. Quoted in Henry F. Pringle, *Theodore Roosevelt: A Biography* (New York: Harcourt, Brace and World, 1956), 418.
2. Quoted in William Roscoe Thayer, *Theodore Roosevelt: An Intimate Biography* (New York: Grosset and Dunlap, 1919), 450.
3. Roosevelt, *Autobiography*, 558.
4. Ibid., 27.
5. Lincoln Steffens, *The Autobiography of Lincoln Steffens* (New York: Harcourt, Brace, 1931), 509, 580.

Bibliography

Bederman, Gail. *Manliness and Civilization: A Cultural History of Gender and Race in the United States, 1880–1917.* Chicago: University of Chicago Press, 1995.

Brown, Richard C. "General Emory Upton—the Army's Mahan." *Military Affairs* 17 (Autumn 1953): 125–31.

Bryce, James. *The American Commonwealth.* Vol. 2, 3rd rev. ed. New York: The Macmillan Co., 1904.

Commager, Henry Steele. *The American Mind: An Interpretation of American Thought and Character since the 1880's.* New Haven: Yale University Press, 1950.

Crunden, Robert M. *Ministers of Reform: The Progressives' Achievement in American Civilization, 1889–1920.* New York: Basic Books, 1982.

Davis, Richard Harding. *Notes of a War Correspondent.* New York: Charles Scribner's Sons, 1914.

Depew, Chauncey M. *My Memories of Eighty Years.* New York: Charles Scribner's Sons, 1924.

DeWitt, Benjamin Parke. *The Progressive Movement.* 1915. Reprint. Seattle: University of Washington Press, 1968.

Dyer, Thomas G. *Theodore Roosevelt and the Idea of Race.* Baton Rouge: Louisiana State University Press, 1980.

Ferguson, Niall. *Colossus: The Rise and Fall of the American Empire.* New York: Penguin Books, 2005.

Foraker, Joseph B. *Notes of a Busy Life.* 3rd ed. Vol. 2. Cincinnati: Stewart and Kidd, 1917.

Gould, Lewis L. *The Presidency of Theodore Roosevelt.* Lawrence: University Press of Kansas, 1991.

———. *The Spanish-American War and President McKinley.* Lawrence: University Press of Kansas, 1980.

———. *Theodore Roosevelt.* New York: Oxford University Press, 2012.

Harbaugh, William H. *The Life and Times of Theodore Roosevelt.* Rev. ed. 1961. New York: Oxford University Press, 1975.

Hays, Samuel P. *The Response to Industrialism, 1885–1914.* 2nd ed. Chicago: University of Chicago Press, 1995.

Headrick, Daniel R. *The Tentacles of Progress: Technology Transfer in the Age of Imperialism, 1850–1940*. New York: Oxford University Press, 1988.

Hendrix, Henry J. *Theodore Roosevelt's Naval Diplomacy: The U.S. Navy and the Birth of the American Century*. Annapolis: Naval Institute Press, 2009.

Hofstadter, Richard. *The Age of Reform: From Bryan to F.D.R.* New York: Knopf, 1955.

Hoganson, Kristin L. *Fighting for American Manhood: How Gender Politics Provoked the Spanish-American and Philippine-American Wars*. New Haven, Conn.: Yale University Press, 1998.

Jones, Howard Mumford. *The Age of Energy: Varieties of American Experience, 1865–1915*. New York: Viking Press, 1971.

Kloppenberg, James T. *Uncertain Victory: Social Democracy and Progressivism in European and American Thought, 1870–1920*. New York: Oxford University Press, 1986.

La Follette, Robert M. *La Follette's Autobiography: A Personal Narrative of Political Experiences*. 1916. Reprint. Madison: University of Wisconsin Press, 1960.

Langley, Lester D. *The Banana Wars: United States Intervention in the Caribbean, 1898–1934*. Wilmington, Del,.: Scholarly Resources, 2002.

Lasch, Christopher. "Editor's Introduction" to Theodore Roosevelt, *The Winning of the West*. Abridged ed. New York: Fawcett, 1963, vii–xv.

Mahan, Alfred Thayer. *The Influence of Sea Power Upon History, 1660–1783*. 1890. Reprint. New York: Barnes & Noble, 2004.

McCulloch, David. *Mornings on Horseback*. New York: Simon and Schuster, 1981.

Miller, Richard H., ed. *American Imperialism in 1898: The Quest for National Fulfillment*. Problems in American History Series. New York: John Wiley and Sons, 1970.

Millis, Walter. *The Martial Spirit*. 1931. Reprint. Chicago: Ivan R. Dee, 1989.

Musicant, Ivan. *Empire by Default: The Spanish-American War and the Dawn of the American Century*. New York: Henry Holt, 1998.

Noble, David F. *America by Design: Science, Technology, and the Rise of Corporate Capitalism*. New York: Oxford University Press, 1977.

O'Toole, G. J. A. *The Spanish War: An American Epic 1898*. New York: W. W. Norton, 1984.
Painter, Nell Irvin. *Standing at Armageddon: The United States, 1877–1919*. New York: W. W. Norton, 1987.
Pisani, Donald J. *To Reclaim a Divided West: Water, Law, and Public Policy, 1848–1902*. Albuquerque: University of New Mexico Press, 1992.
Ponder, Stephen. *Managing the Press: Origins of the Media Presidency, 1897–1933*. New York: Palgrave Macmillan, 2000.
Pringle, Henry F. *Theodore Roosevelt: A Biography*. Rev. ed. 1931. New York: Harcourt, Brace and World, 1956.
Riis, Jacob A. *The Making of an American*. New York: Macmillan, 1902.
———. *Theodore Roosevelt the Citizen*. New York: Grosset and Dunlap, 1903.
Rodgers, Daniel T. *Atlantic Crossings: Social Politics in a Progressive Age*. Cambridge: Harvard University Press, 1998.
Roosevelt, Theodore. "The College Graduate and Public Life." *Atlantic Monthly* 442 (August 1894): 255, 256.
———. *Hunting the Grisly and Other Sketches*. 1889. Reprint. New York: Barnes and Noble, 2003.
———. *The Naval War of 1812: or The History of the United States Navy during the Last War with Great Britain, to Which Is Appended an Account of the Battle of New Orleans*. 2 vols. 1882. Reprint. New York: G. P. Putnam's Sons, 1907.
———. *Ranch Life and the Hunting Trail*. 1888. Reprint. New York: Bonanza Books, 1978.
———. *The Rough Riders*. 1899. Reprint. New York: Barnes and Noble, 2004.
———. *The Strenuous Life: Essays and Addresses*. New York: Century, 1901.
———. *Theodore Roosevelt: an Autobiography*. 1913. Reprint. New York: Da Capo Press, 1985.
———. *The Wilderness Hunter*. 1905. Reprint. New York: Barnes and Noble, 2004.
———. *The Winning of the West*. 4 vols. 1889–1896. Reprint. Lincoln: University of Nebraska Press, Bison Books, 1995.
Rosen, Stephen Peter. "War and the Intellectuals." *American Interest* 8 (January/ February 2013): 41–52.

Samuels, Peggy, and Harold Samuels. *Teddy Roosevelt at San Juan: The Making of a President*. College Station: Texas A&M University Press, 1997.

Smith, Joseph. *The Spanish-American War: Conflict in the Caribbean and the Pacific, 1895–1902*. New York: Longman, 1994.

Steffens, Lincoln. *The Autobiography of Lincoln Steffens*. New York: Harcourt, Brace, 1931.

Stewart, J. C. "Uniforms of the Cowboy Cavalry." In *Rough Writings: Perspectives on Buckey O'Neill, Pauline M. O'Neill, and Roosevelt's Rough Riders*, comp. Janet Lovelady, 64–69. Prescott, Ariz.: Sharlot Hall Museum Press, 1998.

Summers, Mark Wahlgren. *The Gilded Age: or, The Hazard of New Functions*. Upper Saddle River, N.J.: Prentice-Hall, 1997.

Thayer, William Roscoe. *Theodore Roosevelt: An Intimate Biography*. New York: Grosset and Dunlap, 1919.

Trachtenberg, Alan. *The Incorporation of America: Culture and Society in the Gilded Age*. New York: Hill and Wang, 1982.

Upton, Emory. *The Military Policy of the United States*. Washington, D.C.: Government Printing Office, 1912.

Walker, Dale L. *The Boys of '98: Theodore Roosevelt and the Rough Riders*. New York: Tom Doherty Associates, 1998.

Warren, Louis S. *The Hunter's Game: Poachers and Conservationists in Twentieth-Century America*. New Haven: Yale University Press, 1997.

Wheeler, Joseph. *The Santiago Campaign, 1898*. 1898. Reprint. Port Washington, N.Y.: Kennikat Press, 1971.

White, G. Edward. *The Eastern Establishment and the Western Experience: The West of Frederic Remington, Theodore Roosevelt, and Owen Wister*. Austin: University of Texas Press, 1989.

White, Richard. *"It's Your Misfortune and None of My Own": A New History of the American West*. Norman: University of Oklahoma Press, 1991.

Wiebe, Robert H. *The Search for Order, 1877–1920*. New York: Hill and Wang, 1967.

Wilbur, Ray Lyman, and William Atherton Du Puy. *Conservation in the Department of the Interior*. Washington, D.C.: U.S. GPO, 1931.

Wister, Owen. *Roosevelt: The Story of a Friendship, 1880–1919*. New York: Macmillan, 1930.

About the Author

M. DAVID KEY is a native Floridian and a graduate of the University of New Mexico, where he earned a PhD. He taught at the University of New Mexico and the University of Tennessee-Knoxville before taking up small college life as a member of the department of history in Tusculum College, where he teaches U.S. history and political philosophy. He currently resides in Greeneville, Tennessee.

The Naval Institute Press is the book-publishing arm of the U.S. Naval Institute, a private, nonprofit, membership society for sea service professionals and others who share an interest in naval and maritime affairs. Established in 1873 at the U.S. Naval Academy in Annapolis, Maryland, where its offices remain today, the Naval Institute has members worldwide.

Members of the Naval Institute support the education programs of the society and receive the influential monthly magazine *Proceedings* or the colorful bimonthly magazine *Naval History* and discounts on fine nautical prints and on ship and aircraft photos. They also have access to the transcripts of the Institute's Oral History Program and get discounted admission to any of the Institute-sponsored seminars offered around the country.

The Naval Institute's book-publishing program, begun in 1898 with basic guides to naval practices, has broadened its scope to include books of more general interest. Now the Naval Institute Press publishes about seventy titles each year, ranging from how-to books on boating and navigation to battle histories, biographies, ship and aircraft guides, and novels. Institute members receive significant discounts on the Press' more than eight hundred books in print.

Full-time students are eligible for special half-price membership rates. Life memberships are also available.

For more information about Naval Institute Press books that are currently available, visit www.usni.org/press/books. To learn about joining the U.S. Naval Institute, please write to:

Member Services
U.S. Naval Institute
291 Wood Road
Annapolis, MD 21402-5034
Telephone: (800) 233-8764
Fax: (410) 571-1703
Web address: www.usni.org

www.ingramcontent.com/pod-product-compliance
Lightning Source LLC
Chambersburg PA
CBHW031258290426
44109CB00012B/635